When we move our bodies, we move our minds. The grit and determination we summon to best ourselves allows us for greater reflection on the journey . . . not only on the path, but within our lives. We learn more about ourselves through the obstacles we overcome, the people sharing that same sense of purpose, and the world around us, which has given us the opportunity to breathe, to move, and to observe. Running brings us closer to ourselves, the people around us, and the Earth itself. In this book that champions the body, mind, heart, and spirit, those who have challenged (and surprised) themselves share their intimate words detailing their experiences, serving as not only a wellspring of guidance and inspiration but as compelling source material for the motivation for better health.

—Dominic Cottone
  Senior Managing Director of Leadership Consulting
  Expert in Executive Wellness, Ferguson Partners

Chasing Twilight *brings insight with a fresh or forgotten perspective, which will help any runner shape their thoughts with a positive spin.*

—Jim Walmsley
  Professional Ultrarunner

We all have our own personal reasons for running. I believe that all of these reasons collectively add up to one common purpose—that is, to feel good about ourselves . . . physically, mentally, and emotionally. There is nothing more powerful in our lives than our own personal self-esteem and self-confidence as that is the very foundation by which we all accomplish everything else in our lives. Chasing Twilight *captures this very concept in so many compelling and inspiring ways which all of us who run can identify with. Every day is a gift, and the messages and stories in this book are real evidence of this truth. Well done.*

—Dave McGillivray
　Boston Marathon Race Director

The true beauty of running is the journey and adventure it provides. Running inspires self-reflection and sparks personal growth, no matter your pace, talent, or ability. Adam, Jim, and Connor have tapped into this beautiful power of running, and invite the reader to reflect on their own journey as a runner and to remember the child-like joy that we often feel (and forget). Chasing Twilight *is thought-provoking and inspiring, for the new runner to the professional, and will make you fall in love with running all over again.*

—Jill Deering and Monica DeVreese
　Cofounders of rabbit running apparel

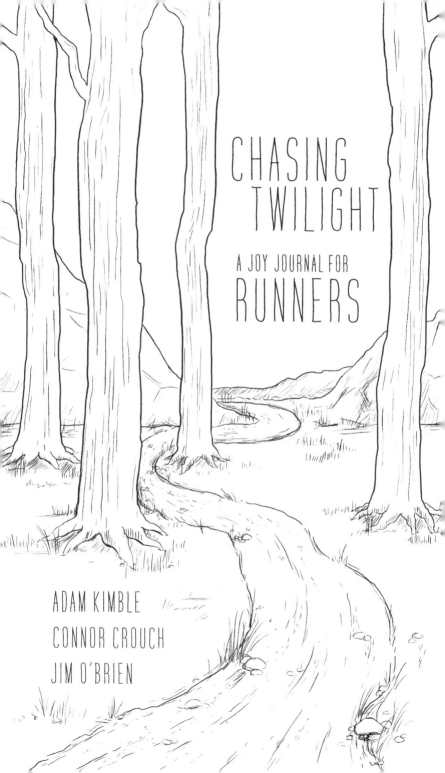

CHASING TWILIGHT

A JOY JOURNAL FOR RUNNERS

ADAM KIMBLE

CONNOR CROUCH

JIM O'BRIEN

Writers of the Round Table Press
PO Box 1603, Deerfield, IL 60015
www.roundtablecompanies.com

Printed in the United States of America

First Edition: October 2021
10 9 8 7 6 5 4 3 2 1

Library of Congress Cataloging-in-Publication Data
Chasing twilight: a joy journal for runners / Adam Kimble,
Connor Crouch, Jim O'Brien.—1st ed. p. cm.
ISBN Paperback: 978-1-61066-096-9
Library of Congress Control Number: 2021940105

Writers of the Round Table Press and the logo
are trademarks of Writers of the Round Table, Inc.

Editor: **James Cook**
Cover Illustration and Designer: **Christy Bui**
Interior Designer: **Sunny DiMartino**
Painting Artist: **Lyndsey Crouch**
Proofreaders: **Adam Lawrence, Sunny DiMartino**

Adam Kimble | *To my wife, Karen, who has been 100 percent committed to every one of my "impossible" goals and given me the flexibility in life to pursue my dream of being a professional ultrarunner. Without your support, none of my accomplishments would be possible.*

And to my longtime friend Mark Smith, who was called home far too soon. You may not be here in body, but your spirit lives on in your family and friends. I will always be a better man because of your love and friendship. RAMM forever and always #SmithStrong, brother.

Connor Crouch | *To Lyndsey, who watched and waited in the wind and rain in Boston (2018) and who has always been my greatest supporter.*

Jim O'Brien | *To Michelle, who has run with me for thousands of miles and who has been my patient crew chief in this ultramarathon called life. Thank you, my love.*

Introduction: Why We Wrote This Book

Adam Kimble | When Jim asked me to be a part of this project, I immediately said "Yes!" Running has not only been a passion and career for me, but it has completely changed me. I often reflect on the thought that I wouldn't truly know who I am if it weren't for the lessons I've learned through my running journey. As such, I make it my daily mission to inspire others, help push themselves past their perceived limits, and determine what they are truly capable of. Whether in running or in life, we all have unique talents, and the greatest gift we can give the world is to utilize them. I hope this journal inspires you and helps you redefine what is possible in your life. *AhK*

Connor Crouch | I love running and writing because they are both challenging activities. They require time and persistence and can often be painful or frustrating. They also offer us a regular opportunity to see how hard work translates to improvement. Finally, running and writing give us a valuable time to observe, reflect, and appreciate the world around us. But as much as I have run *and* written, I had never considered journaling about running until Jim approached me about putting this book together. I'm so grateful he did, because a year of journaling about and reflecting on running has given me a new appreciation for the simple act of getting out my door each day to run. Moreover, reading Adam's and Jim's entries throughout the year has pushed me to become a better and more thoughtful runner and writer. I hope that this journal provides that same inspiration to you. (Though I hope you have a bit more motivation to journal and run every day than I did!) *Con*

Jim O'Brien | I have always wanted to write a book of running reflections, but I couldn't find my vision. I knew what I didn't want: another running logbook full of miles and pace and weather. Instead, I knew I wanted to capture my inner journey and thoughts, but I didn't think that was possible until I read Clare Gallagher's haiku in *Trail Runner Magazine*.[1] The beautiful haiku, called "Ultrarunning," was about "Happy weirdos running all day." I tore it out of the magazine and put it in my office where I would continually look at and reflect on it. The haiku was like a koan for me—this thing that the more I studied, the less I understood, yet, at a gut level, kept calling me. Then one day, like a flash of lightning, I realized the haiku was showing me that it was possible to write poems and essays about the inner journey running was taking me on. While a run is an outer journey, there is also an inner journey—one I wanted to capture and reflect on. I realized I wanted to help others capture their inner running journeys.

Then I recruited my stepson Connor and our friend (and my running coach) Adam Kimble to join me. They are both fantastic runners and wonderful people, and collaborating with them on this journal has been a huge amount of fun. I am richer for our shared journey and grateful for their efforts.

For me, running is the thing that continually refines and inspires me, and I hope the journal will give you the space to do this as well.

I'll see you further on up the road . . .

HOW THE THREE OF US MET

How did the three of us meet? We will have to blame Connor's mom, Michelle, who is also Jim's wife. Michelle, who is a personal trainer, worked with Adam ahead of his transcontinental run across the United States, teaching him techniques for running in a pool. After that, the four of us became friends, and Michelle and Adam and Connor crewed for Jim at his ultramarathons, forming bonds that can only result from staying up all night while waiting for a slow Jim to show up at the next aid station.

In addition to working together on this book, Adam coaches Jim and Michelle for their ultrarun training.

How to Use This Journal

Our objective when creating this journal was to give you the opportunity to reflect and write in whatever way makes the most sense to you. Writing, like running, is a highly individual journey. While we hope that our entries can provide inspiration for you, we have left the area for you to write completely blank. Additional writing space is available at the end of the book. Here are some potential ways in which you can use this journal.

1. USING OUR ENTRIES AS A GUIDE

From short poems to long reflections, our entries vary quite a bit. You could use the last entry you read as a guide for what to write next. This will allow you to experiment with many different forms of writing. If you just read a haiku, how about giving poetry a try? Alternatively, you may not like to write poetry, in which case you can take a theme or concept from our entry and apply it to your reflection. Perhaps the day's entry mentions a neat bird or beautiful view—can you think about a small natural wonder that you observed on today's run?

2. RUNNING LOG

Perhaps you are more quantitative than qualitative. Rather than try to write free verse, you can simply use the blank space as an opportunity to reflect on the nuts and bolts of your run. How far did you go? What was the weather like? How did you feel? You could even use this

journal first thing in the morning before you run at all.
What are you looking forward to seeing today on your
run? If you're really feeling ambitious, you could write
a short entry before *and* after you run to give you some
insight into how the day's run changed your mentality.

3. PEAKS AND VALLEYS

Sometimes it's easier to journal when you have a strict
framework to work within. For example, each day you
could consider what the peaks and valleys, or highs and
lows, of your run were. What was one thing from today
that you hope to remember five years from now? What is
one mistake you made today that you can learn from?

4. GRATITUDE

Many of our entries are focused on the gratitude that
we have for running. To keep things simple, you could
reflect on one thing you were grateful for from the day's
run (or rest day!).

No matter how you choose to use this journal, we
hope that you will find as much value as we did in taking
a moment to reflect each day. Don't beat yourself up if
you miss a day (or week) or two. Just like in running, a
day off to recharge can sometimes be more valuable than
holding yourself to an impossible standard. With that
said, we wish you the best as you begin your running,
reflecting, and writing journey!

PART I
Warm-Up

Autumn

Hazy fall sunlight
Dreamy, golden
Staring out the window
At the still green world
I can't wait to run

— Jim

Ultrarunning

I recently read about the impracticality of ultrarunning (competing in races longer than the traditional marathon length of 26.2 miles) in a modern world. In today's society, with so many technical advances and the ability to travel the globe via machines, the article asked why would someone *run* a hundred miles? My answer: because you don't find out who you are by flying in an airplane or driving in a car.

— *Adam*

DATE

New Runners

Spring turns to summer, bringing new runners shuffling along the sidewalk, grinding their way through a run. These runs are the toughest ones, journeys into a new and unfamiliar world, full of doubt and new aches and pains. These runs are tougher than any ultramarathon, and when I see these new runners, I am inspired to seek their grit within myself. I'll see you further on up the road . . .

— *Jim*

The Choice

Each day we have a choice. To run or not to run?
To do a workout or take an easy day? To do a strength
training session, a stretching routine, or nothing?
The beauty of running is having the power each day to
make a simple choice that will make us a better version
of ourselves. So, what will your choice be?

— *Connor*

DATE

DATE

DATE

DATE

DATE

Time of Day

I know many people prefer to run at the same time on most days, but personally, I like to mix it up. Running at different times is exactly that: different!

In the morning, it's often brisk and quiet, and your body is usually a little more tired; in the afternoon, things are usually a lot busier, the sun is out, and your energy levels are rising. In the evening, the sun is setting, the day is winding down, and there's a strange dichotomy of increasing heart rate and the calm of the dusk. If you ask me, all three give me something different, and as William Cowper reminded us, "Variety is the spice of life."

— *Adam*

DATE

Dream

When the Japanese Zen Master Takuan was on his deathbed, he was asked for his last words. Using brush and ink, he wrote the word "dream." I sometimes wonder what he meant. That life is a dream or an illusion? Or that we should dream and seek to accomplish our dreams? Or had he just awakened from an enlightening dream? We will never know.

Runners have a lot of dreams. We dream of setting personal records, of running so many miles in a week or month or year, and of running specific races. I dream of running across the United States, of doing big runs in the mountains, and of going back to Marin County and running the Dipsea Trail.

There is also today's dream.

Today, on a gray day where the new snow lies on the cold world, I dream of a run where I see a red cardinal in the white woods. I don't control whether this dream comes true, but to give it a chance, I need to get out the door.

— *Jim*

> *PS. Postrun update: I did see a cardinal in the woods. Dreams do come true!*

Control

One of the main tenets of Stoicism is to focus on what's in our control. Easy to say, hard to do!

Applying this to running looks like this:

In my control:
Getting out the door and going for a run
What I wear
How fast or slow I go
How I breathe
What I think about while running

Partially in my control:
What time I run
Who I run with

Not in my control:
The weather
How I feel during the run
A sudden need to use the bathroom

The *aha!* here is how much time I spend thinking about the things not in my control or partially in my control. I have six weather apps and can get lost in them trying to predict the weather. (Not in my control!)

Getting out the door to run is the most important thing within my control. How often do I make sure I do it? A lot to consider here.

I'll see you further on up the road . . .

— *Jim*

DATE

DATE

Trails

The trails that I call home are so diverse. Even after three-plus years of living in Tahoe, there are still so many trails I know about but have yet to explore.

As I continue to glide up and down the mountains, the energy from each trail binds me closer to my home. Connecting one trail I love to run on to another trail I love to run on has been my recent inspiration. Even trails that feel incredibly familiar are surprising me on a daily basis. So my challenge to you today is this: get outside and let your local running spots surprise you!

— Adam

DATE

DATE

DATE

17

DATE

Kid on Christmas

The weather has reached the point in the season where I feel like a kid on Christmas morning.

Here in Tahoe, the trails are melting, and while some are still partially covered in snow, most of them are clear and ready for action. Because of this, deciding where to run each day becomes a fun and exciting game.

Even though I've run on all of these trails before, the first season's run on each is a special experience. Each run, each trail, and each adventure—both new and old—is a beautiful gift.

— *Adam*

Growth

Sometimes, before a run, I am afraid of what lies ahead. Will I struggle? Will I bonk and have to walk home? Will my time be embarrassingly slow?

"Yeah," I tell myself. "But you won't know unless you get out the door and get going. You grow more from the hard days than the easy days." I'll see you further on up the road . . .

— *Jim*

DATE	

DATE

DATE

21

DATE

DATE

New Opportunities

I tell the runners I coach that every day is a new day and a new opportunity for a great run! Sometimes they're struggling with a recent workout or feeling bogged down by the stressors of life. Or they have a bad run and then start feeling anxious or inadequate about achieving their goals.

The fact is this: every run is different, and each new run is a new opportunity! When you see it from this perspective, you realize that a training cycle is filled with lots of good and lots of bad runs. It's your consistency in and commitment to showing up every day that gets you where you're going!

— Adam

DATE

Same Ol' New

Running routes are full of signs and wonders, waiting to be seen. My usual running path winds through our suburb, over a pedestrian walkway crossing a highway, and then into the next town. There is a rise Michelle and I call "Budget Hill" as our private joke. It's short and steep, and we sometimes play a game of trying to get the other person wound up about a subject so they excitedly do all the talking—and breathing—while climbing the hill.

Budget Hill has some old oaks on it. A sharp-shinned hawk lives in one of them. I saw the hawk today just after dawn, struggling in the fierce east wind. It made some harsh calls as it settled into the limbs, and I wondered if the calls were directed at me or something else I could not see.

My morning runs are full of these little landmarks: the place where I once saw a Baltimore oriole, the block where it's wise to watch out for skunks, the construction site with a porta potty (always good to know!). My six-mile path is a blend of the same-old-thing with who-knows-what. Part of the joy of running is going out and searching for the world's beauty.

I'll see you further on up the road . . .

— *Jim*

Warmth

Air ripe with the scent
of dry pine needles. Ah . . .
shorts and t-shirt weather.

— *Connor*

Memories

I tend to reminisce a lot when I run.

Running is such a profoundly impactful activity; with it comes so many memorable experiences. Whether it was a race, an adventure, an expedition, or a run with some friends, my mind carries many great running memories.

Every time I go on another run, those experiences flood my mind and take me through the landmarks of my running journey.

— *Adam*

DATE

DATE

DATE

DATE

DATE

One Run?

Is a run ever just *one* run? Doesn't it frequently seem that one run is really just a collection of a bunch of shorter runs happening within the same time frame?

I feel great!

Nope, I don't feel so great anymore.

I'm bonking!

Whoa, I've got so much energy!

Have I already been running for an hour—it feels like I just started!

When is this going to end?

These stories are formed in the mind, and we must do our best to only entertain the stories that will get us to the finish line, wherever that line may be.

— *Adam*

DATE

Don't Turn None Away

I sometimes attach too much importance to New Year's Day, thinking about all the things I want to do in the new year, including running. This year, 2020, I am thinking about my runs the way Townes Van Zandt wrote about life in his song "To Live Is to Fly." Read these wonderfully poetic lines aloud:

> Days, up and down they come
> Like rain on a conga drum
> Forget most, remember some
> But don't turn none away
> Everything is not enough
> And nothin' is too much to bear
> Where you been is good and gone
> All you keep is the getting there . . .[2]

Runs blur in my mind. Looking back over 2019, I can't remember most of my runs. Sure, I remember the hard ones like a five-hour run in the rain, or a magical May run along Lake Geneva, Wisconsin, with my wife, Michelle, and seeing dozens of migrating birds, including eight scarlet tanagers. I remember an altitude run with Connor, climbing uphill for miles in Flagstaff, and the endless struggle to breathe and not giving in to the craving to walk. But they are mostly all blurred.

"Forget most, remember some / But don't turn none away . . ."[3]

For 2020, I am going to work on not turning any runs away. My determination is the only thing in my control. Getting to this place right now and the chance to run and taking it and being where my feet are, in the moment, under an open sky, and happy to be moving—ever restless yet resting peacefully in the rhythm of my legs. I'll see you further on up the road . . .

— *Jim*

DATE	

Spring Thaw

The spring thaw in Tahoe is an exciting time. If it was a heavy-snow winter, it means the thaw will continue well into June.

This year, the snowfall was light, so many of the trails are opening up in April. And even when I've run on a particular trail countless times, there is still nothing like getting out on it for the first time of the season!

— Adam

DATE _____

_____

_____

_____

_____

_____

_____

_____

_____

_____

_____

_____

_____

_____

_____

_____

_____

DATE

DATE

33

Fleeting

Once, while running, I found some cards on the ground. They were from Alcoholics Anonymous (AA) and had some bible scripture on one side and different steps from AA's Twelve-Step Program on the other side. I picked a couple of them up and kept them—I am not sure why.

One of the scripture quotes was from James 4:14, and it says, "For what is your life? It is even a vapour, that apeareth for a little time and then vanisheth away" (King James Version).

This quote is similar to part of the Diamond Sutra in Buddhism:

> So you should view this fleeting world—
> A star at dawn, a bubble in a stream,
> A flash of lightning in a summer cloud,
> A flickering lamp, a phantom, and a dream.[4]

Our runs are fleeting, shooting stars across the arc of our lives. Take a moment and appreciate them, for they are gone too soon. I'll see you further on up the road . . .

— *Jim*

Only Company

Porch creaks, insects hum . . .
this morning, the moon is my
only company.

— *Connor*

Running Is There

Running so often meets us where we're at. Do we need to get in a run to calm our nerves?

Running is there.

Do we need to clear our mind and think through life?

Running is there.

Do we need to push ourselves and do whatever we can to get better?

Running is there.

Today, I warmed up with a yoga class and then needed a little shakeout to work out the kinks and promote good blood flow to my muscle tissues for maximum recovery.

Guess what?

Running was there.

— *Adam*

DATE

One Great Thing

There's something to be said for waking up before sunrise to run. Feeling like the first person awake in town, being the first to step foot on the trail, and listening as the birds transition from sleep to song. Knowing that no matter what happens the rest of the day, I've done one great thing.

— *Connor*

The Escarpment

I ran up to the top of the Escarpment today. What is that? It's the high point on the Western States 100 course, and it happens a mere three and a half miles into the race.

The race begins in Olympic Valley, where you run up a mountain, crest the top, and then begin the hundred-mile descent to Auburn, California. I ran the race in 2018, and as I ran it again today for fun, I was unintentionally back in my shoes during the race.

There's an electricity about the atmosphere at Western States, and even when I'm running on the course with nobody around, I still feel it. My heart beats with a fiery intensity as if there were thousands of spectators lining the course cheering on runners the way they do on race day every June. It's as if the energy of the race never leaves, and it's up to me to find it. I find a supreme beauty in the memories we attach to specific trails and roads we've run on before. Today, I felt those memories bubbling to the surface like never before!

— *Adam*

DATE

DATE

Weather

To the modern American, weather is little more than an inconvenience and a bad topic for small talk. But to runners, weather is a subject of intense scrutiny and consideration. Weather grounds us to the everyday whims of the world in which we live.

Like farmers, sailors, and mushroom hunters, we have a close relationship with yesterday's snow, today's rain, and tomorrow's forecast. Ultimately, we learn that the weather is out of our control. We appreciate the good days, and we treat the bad days as an opportunity to strengthen ourselves.

As for me, I hope that tomorrow will be sunny and sixty!

— *Connor*

DATE

_____

_____

_____

_____

_____

_____

_____

_____

_____

_____

_____

_____

_____

Bad Short-Term Memory

Runners tend to have what I like to call "bad short-term memory." Once the agony of a race or a run subsides, we find ourselves reminiscing about all of the highs and the accomplishments that came along with the pursuit of our goals.

You might think, "Why am I doing this?" during the race, as the ache of muscular fatigue commands your mind and becomes your solitary focus. Then later on, all you think about is the elation that came with crossing the finish line. Wouldn't it be special if the whole world could do this? Forget the bad, focus on the positives!

— *Adam*

Sniffing the Air

We have two Yorkies. When they go outside to go to the bathroom, the first thing they do is pause for an instant and sniff the air. Dogs have much more sensitive noses than we do, and in a sense, the world speaks to them through their noses.

For me, running is like a dog's sniffing. I experience the world, feeling how it has changed since yesterday. I also feel myself; what's the same, what's different. When I don't run, I feel disconnected from both the world and myself.

I'll see you further on up the road . . .

— *Jim*

DATE

DATE

Running Is a Mirror

Running is a mirror. It shows me how weak or strong my body is and shows me my emotions: What am I struggling with? What do I feel good about? What problem do I need to turn over in my mind while my legs churn forward?

If I look closely in that mirror, I also see my obsessions: Am I hung up on my pace or miles for the week? Am I going over and over some little issue that has no importance in the greater scheme of life?

Look in the mirror. What do you see?

I'll see you further on up the road . . .

— *Jim*

DATE

Hawk Surprise

After enduring a week of snow, followed by rain that froze into ice, and then even more snow, the treacherous conditions shut me out of running in the woods and trails. These conditions marked out the true start of winter, the long slog when only the streets are available.

Around mile five on this first winter street run, I spotted a red-tailed hawk that had just taken off from a tree in someone's yard. The hawk was perfectly camouflaged for winter hunting, its plumage splashed with irregular blobs of white and gray. It looked magnificent. But then it dipped behind some trees and was lost to sight.

Every run has the potential for surprise like the hawk. But to get the surprise, you have to do the run. It's good to remind myself of that; I have to get outside and start running to see the world and its often hidden but never-ending beauty.

I'll see you further on up the road . . .

— *Jim*

Spring's Leaves

Spring's new leaves stretching out
in the brisk morning air . . .
my legs do the same.

— *Connor*

Hitting the Pavement … Again

I used to run exclusively on pavement, but once I turned professional in ultrarunning, I began running almost exclusively on trails. I love the remoteness and beauty of trails, and my passion for running in the wilderness was clear.

But as I write this, the COVID-19 virus pandemic is spreading, and we are embracing social distancing actions. These, plus a recent string of big snowstorms in Tahoe, mean I'm pretty much relegated to running only on pavement for the time being. While it's certainly not my preference, it does remind me of what brought me into this sport. I can't help but express gratitude and happiness as I reflect on my unlikely journey to a life of ultrarunning.

— *Adam*

DATE

DATE

DATE

DATE

DATE

That Thing

When I started first grade, my Dad brought me to school for an introduction. I remember sitting in the classroom and watching from the window as Dad receded into the distance across the playground. I didn't know if he was coming back, and I knew I didn't want to be in that classroom.

For the next twenty years of school, that feeling of not wanting to be there never changed. That feeling continued when I joined the working world. I have always been buffeted by a yearning to be outside under the wide-open sky, a restlessness to be moving and to be seeing new things.

Running connects me to this ravenous thing inside of me, and I keep coming back for more. The next run, the next mini adventure, the next glimpse of the world's beauty.

I'll see you further on up the road . . .

— Jim

DATE

Night Owl's Curse

I got up to run today at 5:00 a.m. and was back in bed by 5:10 a.m.

Michelle, who was already up and ready to teach a group exercise class, suggested, "If you're tired, you should run in the evening."

As a night owl, it takes very little to persuade me to go back to bed, and so I did.

Going back to sleep without running is great until I get up and face the hours of wondering throughout the day whether I will run in the evening. This is a well-worn path for me, going back decades. Many times, life and my laziness get in the way of an evening run.

But just before I left for work, I saw a colleague's email that made me realize I could work from home for a bit, sneak in a run, and then head to the office. Suddenly the gray, gloomy morning looked like rainbows and unicorns, and soon I was running, dodging snowflakes, and feeling like I had already won the day.

I'll see you further on up the road . . .

— *Jim*

Running Memories

Running serves as a function of memory for me in the same way music does. I'll often hear a song and be brought right back to a specific time and place.

In the same way, when I think of places I've been, my mind always jumps to my memories of running in those places. Running is the lens through which I see the world.

— *Adam*

A Dirty Secret

The dirty little secret about running is that it requires sacrifice. As with everything in life, there are positives and negatives. The negatives include time away from friends or family, getting out of a warm bed too soon, and giving up other leisure activities.

The positives include feeling better about yourself, becoming fitter, and getting in tune with your body. There are also feelings of joy, wonder, and curiosity.

I ran in the cold dark today at 5:30 a.m. I was sacrificing sleep and working against my body's natural rhythm of being a *night owl*. I ran six miles, struggled to find a rhythm, and eventually conceded it would be a slow run.

I kept an eye out for skunks where I sometimes see them and heard an early-bird cardinal stirring in the shadows. We were kin in that moment, both up too early.

As I sometimes do, I finished the run at Starbucks, rewarding myself with a giant dark coffee. I walked home under the smiling dawn, happy with today's sacrifices.

— *Jim*

DATE

DATE

57

Go Deeper

How do you get to know someone deeply? There are many ways, but I've found running to be one of the most effective.

When we're running, we let down our walls, allow the endorphins to fill our body, and remove our inhibitions. I've gotten to know some of my best friends most deeply out on a run. There's an unspoken camaraderie, an acknowledgment that the space is safe and what you say to one another is sacred. It's like therapy among friends.

After running with a friend, I'm always reminded of the fact that we are in this thing called life, *together*!

— *Adam*

| DATE |

_____

_____

_____

_____

_____

_____

_____

_____

_____

_____

_____

_____

_____

Simply Grateful

So much is out of our control in this COVID-19 pandemic and in life. Today, I'm grateful to run.

In the small picture, many people who enjoy weightlifting, Pilates, and other indoor fitness activities can't do them right now. Running is one of the few things I can still do, and I'm so grateful for that.

In the big picture, I'm healthy enough to run. We still don't know the long-term effects of COVID-19 or how many of us will contract the disease. But today, I can be grateful for my health and that of my family and friends.

— *Connor*

Running to Meet Me

Sometimes I run to meet myself. Some other version of myself, more complete and better formed. I sometimes imagine I will see Better Jim loping toward me down a hill and we will merge, and I will become the me I've always wanted to be.

It hasn't happened yet.

So I soldier on, running toward Better Jim and pondering what he will look like when I see him coming down that long hill. It's a joyful journey, and I'll see you and Better Jim further on up the road . . .

— *Jim*

DATE

DATE

DATE

63

Decisions

I am heading to my local polling place to vote in the primary. After casting my ballot, I'll head to the trails to run. What if instead of voting for a politician, I was voting for my favorite trail to run on? That would be a much harder decision!

— *Adam*

DATE

Keep Going

Running can be an exercise in stubbornness. Whether it's your first time running around the block or you are running ten miles, both can feel awful. Your body keeps telling you to stop, and your mind and body begin a wrestling match:

Stop, you idiot! This feels horrible. Why are you doing this?

No, keep running—it will feel better soon.

How about if I walk?

Try again tomorrow, this wasn't meant to happen today.

And if in that moment your mind pins your body, wins the match, and you continue running, it's still hard and your body continues chirping at you:

What are you thinking?

Feel that ache and pain? That means stop!

Yet you plod on.

And it might be a perfectly awful run, but you feel better at the end because you found a way to keep going.

"To keep going." There's a lot to reflect on in those three words.

I'll see you further on up the road . . .

— *Jim*

_____

_____

_____

_____

_____

_____

_____

_____

_____

_____

_____

_____

_____

_____

_____

_____

Raw

Waking up to a cold, rainy morning,
I want to stay inside with a warm cup of
    coffee and read,
but what if it rains all day?

— *Connor*

Springtime

Springtime is a promise
Birds chirping and flowers in bloom
Melting snow leaves behind the imprint
   of winter
Shining sun and blue skies propel us
   forward
A delicate balance, past and future,
Culminating in the present.

— *Adam*

DATE

DATE

For the Joy

The world is locked down because of COVID-19, and every running event is canceled for the foreseeable future.

Not having races to train for has been both a curse and a blessing. On the one hand, I'm running much less now than I was before because I don't have anything on the calendar to train for.

On the other hand, I've found a different motivation to get out the door most days.

For perhaps the first time in my life, I'm running solely for the joy of running. I know the run I did today won't really make me faster in whatever marathon or ultra I do after the pandemic ends. But I know that it made me happy to run simply for the sake of running. And today, that's good enough for me.

— *Connor*

DATE

Teamwork

For an "individual sport," running sure is all about the team! Whether it's a running partner, your running club, your crew at a race, or your friends cheering for you virtually and tracking you during your race, the team aspect of this individual sport is so heartfelt and uplifting.

During my first international stage race in the Gobi Desert in 2015, runners were able to go to the media tent after finishing up each day and read messages from friends and loved ones.

As I shuffled gingerly around the campsite, my body was riddled with the fatigue of back-to-back-to-back long days of running through unforgivingly hot desert. But when I got to the computer station and read the encouraging words from my crew spread all over the world, I could practically feel the fatigue melting away. The act of reading their words lit a fire under me and filled me with more strength and determination than I ever could have conjured up on my own. Ultimately, the presence of my team from afar was what propelled me to my first international victory.

— *Adam*

_____

_____

_____

_____

_____

_____

_____

_____

_____

_____

Garden Like a Runner

If I am not running, I might be in the garden. I enjoy gardening and the mistakes and corrections that go along with realizing my vison. For me, it's like painting with materials that are continually evolving and changing.

Running is a bit like gardening. The continuing challenges of trying to plant myself in my running shoes and then meeting whatever the run brings: the weather, my body, my mind. And just like gardening, running is a series of mistakes and corrections: going out too fast, going out too slow, what I eat, when I eat, running too much or running too little.

Like gardening, running is fresh every day, a mystery and a wonder, a chance to enter a world that is both familiar and strange and one that helps me evolve and grow. I'll see you further on up the road . . .

— *Jim*

Longing for Long

Having returned to the working world after a brief time soul searching at home, I am missing Michelle, daylight, and long runs.

There is something inside of me that loves to run for a long way. How long is "long"? Probably ten miles or more. There is something about going long that comforts my inner restlessness and feeds my need to be outside and moving.

When Michelle told a friend of hers that I was training to run one hundred miles, her friend exploded indignantly, "What is he running from?"

For me the real question is what am I running toward?

I don't know, but I'll see you further on up the road and let you know . . .

— Jim

DATE _____

_____

_____

_____

_____

_____

_____

_____

_____

_____

DATE

DATE

75

DATE

DATE

Treadmill

The treadmill.

> Do you hate it?

> Many do.

> I'm usually not a big fan. But here's the thing: it's still a vehicle for doing what I love!

> So, would I rather be outside in the woods?

> Every time.

> But that doesn't change the fact that I can appreciate the treadmill for what it is!

— *Adam*

DATE _____

_____

_____

_____

_____

_____

_____

_____

_____

_____

_____

_____

Wonder Bread

When I was a kid, there was a brand of bread called Wonder Bread. Its slogan was "Helps build strong bodies twelve ways," meaning the bread was enriched with nutrients. There was nothing better for dinner on a hot summer's night than BLTs (bacon, lettuce, and tomato sandwiches) with mayo on Wonder Bread and some potato chips.

Although the idea of enriched foods has fallen out of favor, I like the idea of doing things that make me stronger.

I have a favorite twelve-mile route I call Wonder Bread because its never-ending, rolling hills build my strength and endurance in twelve different ways. I ran it today for the first time in a couple of months, and it felt great to embrace its challenge. As always it was a struggle, but I know it will make me stronger, and that keeps me coming back for more Wonder Bread.

I'll see you further on up the road . . .

— *Jim*

TIP

When you're looking at purchasing a new pair of running shoes, it's best to head to a local running store and try on several pairs. No two pairs of feet are the same, so figure out what works for you instead of relying on advice from others.

_____

_____

_____

_____

_____

_____

_____

_____

_____

_____

_____

_____

Barriers Fall

Running with my partner is such a soul-filling experience.

When I run with my wife, Karen, we tend to have incredible conversations about life! We talk about our hopes and dreams, plan adventures, and discuss our emotions that we might not otherwise share. Running together is the perfect chance to have a one-on-one, distraction-free discussion. Not only does it connect us on a deeper level, but it fills our souls with the wild and free movement that we all need.

Barriers fall, and our hearts open wide. If you haven't run with your partner before, I encourage you to give it a try.

— *Adam*

The New Us

5:30 a.m. and we set out in the cold dark

Wearing headlamps and facemasks

Reminding us of the run

When a driver mistook us

For a SWAT team

This path is a well-worn friend;

We know its icy spots

And where we might see a skunk

Yet each step changes who we are

We run to find the new us

Waiting for that instant

When we stop our watches

And walk east into the rising sun

— *Jim*

DATE

DATE

Different Every Time

I'm constantly in awe of how different every run is, even when you run in a familiar place. Due to the snow in Tahoe, I've been relegated to running on the bike path more frequently since it gets plowed. Meanwhile, the trails are entrenched in deep snow. Whether you are running in the morning or at night, in the sun or in the rain, fast or slow, it's different every time. Running is so straightforward, yet so nuanced.

— Adam

DATE

DATE

_____

_____

_____

_____

_____

_____

_____

_____

_____

_____

_____

_____

_____

_____

_____

_____

Perspective

Perspective is so powerful. When you run, how you run, and at what point in your training you run can make such a difference in how you perceive the run. I felt that today. A typical interval-style workout with a little bit of gear-shifting to test out the legs. Just ten days after the Tarawera one-hundred-miler, a run like this couldn't have felt better. Did I feel perfect? Certainly not. Was I grateful for my body's ability to recover so quickly? Absolutely!

— *Adam*

Companions

Among other things, I am an executive coach, and a new client who knows I run suggested we do a running coaching session. His suggestion reminded me of the Irish saying "Two shorten the road." I have had many great conversations while running, including a million with my wife Michelle. I have also had great conversations with my pacers during an ultramarathon (thank you Colleen, Michelle, Adam, and Connor!).

As much as I enjoy sometimes running alone, there is something special about having a companion to share the road with as the miles drop away. A running companion is one of the great unsung benefits of running.

I'll see you further on up the road . . .

— *Jim*

| DATE |

Purpose of a Run

Running always serves a purpose. Sometimes it's a way to get fit, a fun activity to do with friends, a way to challenge yourself or become the best version of yourself. For me, each individual run represents something different.

Today, I was running for the first time since running the Tarawera one-hundred-miler a few days prior. All I wanted to do was to check in on my body and appreciate the beauty of Queenstown, New Zealand. That was my purpose. But all I could think about was gratitude— gratitude to be able to have a career I love, run in some of the most beautiful places on planet Earth, and be blessed with a body that allows me to do so.

The purpose of each run is ever-changing. It may start as one thing and evolve into another . . . just like the journey of running or the journey of life!

— *Adam*

| DATE |

Running or Writing?

I am an avid reader. When I was in school, I couldn't wait to graduate because then I'd be able to read what I wanted instead of the assigned reading. This seemed to be one of the great privileges of becoming an adult.

This was such a milestone for me that I remember the first few books I read after graduation. One was a book on running called *Meditations from the Breakdown Lane* by James E. Shapiro. It's about his solo run across the United States during the early 1980s. Though I wasn't a runner at the time, the book fascinated me. Running across the United States seemed fearsome and fantastic and something I have thought about since then.

Recently I bought another copy of *Meditations*. And while I still love the idea of running across the US, I now see Shapiro's second challenge: writing a book about it. I wonder which was tougher for him, the running or the writing? This is partly why I am writing this journal—for the challenge of writing well about running. It's not quite like running across the US, but baby steps!

I'll see you further on up the road . . .

— *Jim*

DATE

DATE

89

DATE

DATE

Mentality

Mentality is everything. It's funny how sometimes we can go out for a really long run and feel like the miles are clicking by, and at other times we can have a short, easy run planned, and it feels like it will never end.

More so than anything else, I believe that is the by-product of our mental outlook. Are we excited about the run? It's likely to go well. Are we dreading it? It's probably going to be a sufferfest.

Our mind doesn't always respond to obstacles the way we hope it will, but putting ourselves into uncomfortable positions is how we train it to listen more often. Harness the mind to win the battle!

— *Adam*

Leap into the Unknown

It's funny how trails can be incredibly familiar and yet still contain so many secrets.

As I was running on a familiar trail today, I ran past a connector trail that I've seen many times before. On previous occasions, I either had a preplanned route or was running out of time and didn't take the unknown trail.

Today, I made it happen!

The trail led to an overlook. As I approached the snowy rocks along the ledge, my gaze shifted down to beautiful Prosser Reservoir below. From this isolated pocket on a sunny but cloud-filled day, I had a panoramic view of snow-capped mountains surrounding a seemingly untarnished, glistening body of blue water.

Take the leap into the unknown . . . it will most assuredly result in something inspiring!

— *Adam*

DATE

DATE

DATE

Today's Run

Today's run and I
Sit on the south-facing deck
Growing sleepy in the winter sun
We debate napping
While brown leaves
Finally flown from the oak
Make leaf angels in the slush
Here we go

— *Jim*

DATE

Breaking Hard

> *The world breaks everyone and afterward*
> *many are strong at the broken places.*
> —Ernest Hemingway[5]

One of the things I love about running is how it breaks me. It leads me right up to my edges and sometimes over them. Can I get up early and run today? Can I do the workout? Can I run far? Can I work through this pain?

Last November, during a hundred-mile race, I broke. For six months leading up to it, I had thought about not breaking, and then during the race, I broke quickly. My legs were shattered; I had a persistent leg cramp and had no will left to push forward. But at the next aid station, my crew put me back together. "It will get better," Coach Adam Kimble said. "Your legs will come around." Back on the course, I found to my amazement that he was right.

Am I stronger in the broken places after that hundred-mile race? I don't know. I am humbled at how easily I both broke and was repaired. Our minds are stronger and, at the same time, weaker than we realize. Each run is a lesson in strength and weakness, a gift showing us where our edges lie and how they evolve, day by day.

I'll see you further on up the road . . .

— Jim

DATE

Morning Cold

It's 5:27 a.m. and 34 degrees. My breath comes out,
hangs in the air a moment before being whipped away
by the west wind. My stomach is growling; my knee—
achy and swollen. But I am grateful to be running, out
in the dark, my headlight bobbing. I'll see you further
on up the road . . .

— *Jim*

PART II
Tempo

DATE

DATE

Geese

Do the geese overhead
Wish
They could run?

— *Jim*

Run Instead

"I wouldn't even want to drive a hundred miles!"

Ever heard that before? To be fair, I often agree with that sentiment.

That's why I run instead.

— *Adam*

This Is Nothing

In running, how you frame your situation is everything. If you've run a hundred miles before, and you're out on a long run, you can say to yourself, "Remember that time I ran a hundred miles? This is *nothing* compared to that!"

When you're feeling tired on a normal day, you might think, "I'm not actually tired—tired is when I'm ninety miles into a one-hundred-mile race!"

These sorts of mental games have become invaluable to me. They help me to reframe my struggles and push through obstacles and barriers.

As part of a vertical challenge for my coaching team today, I summited a mountain wearing a (Teenage Mutant Ninja Turtles) Leonardo onesie. The temperature was about seventy-five degrees Fahrenheit, and the suit made it feel so much hotter. Thankfully, I've run in races like the Desert Ultra in Namibia, where temperatures reached as high as 130 degrees!

So guess what I told myself today when I was drenched in sweat underneath my Leo costume? "Hey, remember that time you ran through one of the hottest deserts on earth? This is *nothing* compared to that!"

— *Adam*

DATE

DATE

DATE

Glissading

Mud glissading. Is that a real thing? I found out today.

As I made my way downhill on the muddy trails of Reno, I began sliding down the mountain without moving my feet. I took out my phone to capture this "mudslide." The slickness endured until I fell to the ground and the phone was launched from my hand high into the air. Mother Nature humbled me, letting me know that if I'm going to become any good at mud glissading, I'd better concentrate!

— *Adam*

DATE

The Track

Speed work on a track is a fun workout for me. While I much prefer running on trails in the woods, there's a sacredness about running four-hundred-meter laps around a track, knowing that so many before me have done the same.

It's painful yet therapeutic.

It's monotonous yet exciting.

It's repetitive yet unique.

What beautiful dichotomies!

— *Adam*

DATE

Waits Below

Blue sky and red rocks . . .
an ocean of open air
waits below the rim.

— *Connor*

DATE

Faith and Hard Work

As I write this, it's the beginning of Lent. For me, it serves as a reminder that, when we put our minds to something, we're always capable of much more than we think.

Jesus fasted for forty days and forty nights in the desert, so why can't I push a little harder on this run? Why can't I go a little longer when my mind and body tell me not to?

Three years ago, I competed on Discovery Channel's survival reality show *The Wheel*. I was in the wilderness for sixty days, surviving six different ecozones across South America. My journey on the show was inspired by my friend Mark Smith, who at the time was battling stage 4 brain cancer. The show was the most emotionally, mentally, physically, and spiritually grueling challenge I've ever done. Nearly every day, I thought about giving up and going home, but my faith in God and thoughts of Mark battling for his life kept me going and ultimately led me to victory.

I rely on those memories from the most physically and mentally difficult time of my life to push me further in races and training. When I want to stop, I remind myself that I've been through worse, and I can keep going. With faith and hard work, anything is possible!

— *Adam*

Big Bowl

Like winter cherry blossoms
Snow tumbles from branches
Moving slowly up Big Bowl
We smile

— *Jim*

Every Step

The nighttime darkness
Closing in on my every step
As the light draws near

— Adam

DATE

DATE

113

Another One Arises

Running never gets easier. As you gain more experience, the challenge evolves.

As a beginner, the challenges are choosing to run each day and having the mental and physical strength to do the run.

As a more experienced runner, you are challenged by the trial of miles—knowing that today holds seven, or ten, or twenty miles. And so will tomorrow and the day after that, until one day you've conquered that challenge and another one arises.

— Connor

DATE

DATE

DATE

_____

_____

_____

_____

_____

_____

_____

_____

_____

_____

_____

Running (Snow) Shoes

Have you ever worn or run in snowshoes before? Since moving to Lake Tahoe in 2016, I've become a "snowshoe runner." I love it, because it's yet another way to explore my beloved trails in the winter. And while I enjoy other winter sports like snowboarding and skiing, I don't do them nearly as much as my nearby friends do.

I'm an ultrarunner at heart, and nothing makes me happier. The pairing of trail running and the snow is an awesome compromise for me, a guy who likes the snow but likes running so much more!

Some people ask, "Why not just ski?" But when you love trail running the way I do, you'll find a way to do it, even in the winter months.

— _Adam_

Mixed Emotions

Today's training run was a speed workout, which always makes me feel a plethora of emotions before and after I run. Before the run, I am usually thinking about getting my mind into "attack mode," so I can go out and run hard. It takes more bandwidth than an easy run. At the same time, I also usually have the "this is going to hurt" thoughts, because I know I will be uncomfortable for much of the workout.

The feelings after are always a combination of satisfaction and happiness. I reflect on my ability to push my body and run fast, making myself a better runner and improving my fitness.

— *Adam*

DATE _____

_____

_____

_____

_____

_____

_____

_____

_____

_____

_____

_____

DATE

DATE

Jingles All the Way

If you're a distance runner, at some point somebody has probably asked you, "What do you think about when you're running for such long periods of time?" For me, sometimes I think about everything going on in my life, or other times I think about nothing at all.

Today's thinking was super random: I thought about a math assignment I had in third grade where we had to turn the multiplication tables into jingles. The jingle I remember crafting was "Eight times five equals forty, there is a movie with a pig named Gordy!"

Running sure has a way of "jogging" the memory.

— *Adam*

DATE

Different Strokes

Runners come in all shapes and sizes as do their preferred ways of running. Some runners prefer to run alone; others want a companion. Some must have music; others *never* listen to music.

This summer I have noticed a new category of runner: the phone runner. This runner runs while talking on the phone (via a headset). Sometimes these runners are moving barely above a walking pace, and other times they are sprinting. In some ways, it is no different than running with a companion, but I wonder how it is for the person on the other end of the phone. Is it hard to listen to the rapid breathing? Does it make the listener feel lazy?

When I see a phone runner, I tend to have a knee-jerk reaction of "how could you even consider that?" But then I consider how my dad refused to own a TV until my grandmother sent us one. (He thought they were bad for your mind, although once it arrived at our house, he was happy to watch football games!)

Though for me, I like the solitude of a run and the opportunity to listen to my own thoughts. No song is as sweet as that of my own mind!

I'll see you further on up the road . . .

— *Jim*

DATE

Dog's Life

Ah to be a dog!
Excited for every run
no matter the day.

— *Connor*

DATE

DATE

125

Endurance

Paradoxically, some of the world's oldest trees live in the harshest environments. For example, the bristlecone pines, which can live for nearly five thousand years, grow at high elevations on dry, rocky mountaintops and ridges in California. Similarly, the most resilient runners—and humans in general—are those who have weathered many challenges and have embraced tough workouts, races, and injuries as opportunities to improve.

Like bristlecone pines, we endure. We take that next step, do that last interval, and run that twenty-sixth mile. Not because it's easy, but because it's worth it.

— *Connor*

DATE

DATE

DATE

Gratitude

Gratitude is something I try to practice as often as possible. It helps give me perspective.

Today, I ran one of my local loops I run quite often. I was feeling less than inspired by my typical route, because it wasn't something new and exciting. The funny thing is, just weeks ago when the snowpack was thawing, I was thrilled by the idea of running these trails again. Now that there are so many great running options available, the right-out-the-front-door option is less appealing.

So as I got out on some of my favorite trails, I reflected on how grateful I am to have these trails available to me on a daily basis. It's natural to want to run on a new and exciting trail every day, but that doesn't mean we can't fully appreciate the "usual" that has been so good to us.

— *Adam*

DATE

Two Times in a Day

One of the things I love about running is that it always presents us with new challenges and opportunities to achieve amazing goals. Today, I accomplished something I had never accomplished before: I ran two times on the same day, on different continents, and halfway across the world from one another. I started with a morning run in New Zealand, crossed the international date line on my flight home, and then finished with a night run in Lake Tahoe.

Why?

Why not!

— *Adam*

DATE

The Bond of Running

Tattoos are very popular right now. I am not sure why. Perhaps it's because, in our humanness, we desire to belong to a larger group, and having a tattoo makes us part of one group.

As a runner, it's hard to represent yourself as part of a group unless you are running. But when you are running and you see another runner, there is a bonding moment. We see each other and know we are in this thing together, out on the road, moving, and seeking. This bond is special because we share the effort, the struggle, and the joy of running.

So next time you see a fellow runner, give them a nod or a wave. We are traveling this road together.

I'll see you further on up the road . . .

— Jim

DATE

Energy

How often does the day you're having mimic your energy toward your run?

For me, it can be fairly often. If I'm not feeling stoked about the day, I'm probably not superenergized to run.

Today I spoke to the teams at the 2020 Cross Country Junior National Championships—over four hundred incredibly talented young athletes filled with hope and excitement. So while I was there to inspire them at the Opening Ceremony, I in turn was inspired by their energy, which surged around me. It was palpable!

I took that energy and harnessed it into my run later that day. I was fired up, and it made for a great run.

The question then becomes, how do you do find energy when your day isn't filled with inspiration? You must find a way to create your own, whether it's internal or external. A runner without a purpose, without a "why," is a runner with no chance when the challenges arise. Find your motivation and let it guide you!

— *Adam*

Alone

Alone on the hillside
Running above the city
Dirt scattering under foot
Nature is a silent but reliable partner

— *Adam*

DATE

135

Racing the Rain

Racing the rain, I
watch as the dark clouds build . . .
who will make it home first?

— *Connor*

DATE

DATE

137

Deep Satisfaction

I planned on doing strides toward the end of my easy run today, but when the time came, my legs still felt clunky from this past weekend's fast long run. Rather than beating myself up over my slow recovery or being disappointed that I didn't feel as good as I'd hoped to, I chose to take deep satisfaction from knowing that I'm pushing my body to the edge of its limits.

— *Connor*

DATE

DATE

Rainy Arizona

It's been an unusually rainy and cloudy week in Flagstaff, Arizona. Maybe the long stretches of sunny days have started to spoil me, but I've found myself dreading the thought of getting out in the rain to run.

Today I put off my run until the afternoon and managed to catch a lucky nook between storms. I ran the first thirty minutes without rain and had only a drizzle in the last thirty. I had Buffalo Park largely to myself and enjoyed watching the clouds roll over Elden and the Peaks. It was an enjoyable run on an otherwise gloomy day and made me grateful to have had a reason to get out and enjoy the afternoon.

— *Connor*

DATE

The Other Side of the Mountain

There is a small mound off the highway between Chicago and St. Louis. I always forget where it is until I see it rising up out of the flat prairie. My theory is it's an Indian mound. Each time I drive past it, I promise myself I'll get off the highway and explore it on the next trip. But then forget about the mound until the next time I see it.

But if I were running, I would stop to explore the mound. When I run, there is always time to stop and explore. Running brings me to the other side of the mountain. And there is always another side of the mountain. I'll see you further on up the road . . .

— *Jim*

DATE

DATE

DATE

143

DATE

DATE

What Works

We live in a status-obsessed world. Our clothes, our cars, and the lives we present on social media all send signals about the groups to whom we either belong or aspire to belong.

Runners are different, however. With the exception of those wearing Boston Marathon jackets (and congratulations to you!), runners just care about what works.

Yesterday on a nine-mile run, Michelle and I saw at least fifty runners out in the snow. Some wore shorts and sweatshirts, while others had on facemasks and heavy jackets. Everyone was wearing what worked for them. Full stop.

As we go about the rest of our lives, we should aspire to bring our running ethos into what we do, focusing a bit more on what works and a little less on status.

— Jim

DATE

Wind Factor

When I was a teenaged caddy, I learned that golfers account for the direction and speed of the wind when choosing which club to hit. Sometimes they toss a few blades of grass into the air to see which way the wind is blowing.

Running in Chicago during the winter also involves factoring in the wind. I look at a weather app for the temperature and something called "real feel," which is what the temperature feels like when including the wind. I then decide whether I will wear a heavy or light jacket, whether I need to wear long underwear, and how heavy a shirt I should wear. If the wind is strong, I will run into it to avoid getting chilled or even hypothermia.

Traveling across the wide-open lands west of Chicago, the wind punches me one, two, three, four, as soon as I step outside. It finds every weakness: my sleeves, my neck, the hem of my coat. The battle begins, me pushing forward and the wind pushing back. Our war will last for months until one evening in April, when the daylight lasts a little longer, and then suddenly I realize I no longer have to factor in the wind. But even on those early spring runs, if I listen hard, I can hear the wind saying, "I'll see you further on up the road."

— *Jim*

Olympians

Today was the Olympic Marathon Trials! The day was filled with hope, dreams, joy, disappointment, and struggle.

Some runners had their day.

Many didn't.

Victory comes in many forms, and I hope every runner had their own personal victory today, regardless of the time on the clock. Becoming a better person is often about enduring the trials and tribulations . . .

— *Adam*

More Than I Think

Michelle and I are on a diet this month. It's called the Whole30 and calls for no alcohol, sugar, grains, legumes, or dairy. I am a picky eater who hates vegetables and eggs (See? Picky!), and I never thought I could do this diet. Frankly, I was dreading it, partly because of the limited choices but also because I am independent and resist being told what to do.

At the same time, we also decided to do intermittent fasting, which is fasting for a number of hours each day. One of my biggest concerns was how this would affect my running. Could I actually run on an empty stomach? The answer was yes.

There have been some runs that were a grind without fuel in my system, but I have since come out the other side and am discovering it's okay to run five or six miles at 5:30 a.m. without having eaten anything.

Running offers many lessons. A big one for me is learning that I am capable of more than I think I am. Whether it's with running, or dieting, or whatever challenge I am facing, I am always able to give more than I thought possible.

I'll see you further on up the road . . .

— *Jim*

Ol' Familiar Road

Running down that ol' familiar road
Sure to see things new and old
Jacket off, I feel the cold
Running down that ol' familiar road

— *Adam*

Rhythm of the World

Running reconnects me to the rhythms of the world. When I run outdoors (my strong preference), I feel as if I can sense the earth slowly moving day after day.

Seeing the first birds of spring, the days lengthening toward summer solstice, and the first leaves turning in the fall makes me feel as if I'm running in step with Mother Nature. In northern Illinois where I live, the cardinals singing at daybreak is the first sign of spring. As I finished my run this morning, I heard the first February song of the cardinal. It cheered me because it means we are slightly closer to spring. Hearing the cardinal and feeling the earth tiptoe toward the sun was special.

I'll see you further on up the road . . .

— *Jim*

| DATE |

Focus

Your focus determines your reality.

—Qui-Gon Jinn, *Star Wars Episode I: The Phantom Menace*

I do almost all my running alone. There's no music, podcasts, or even company to distract my mind. Although there are times when I wish I could indulge in a podcast or have a partner to pass the miles with, I embrace the challenge of having nothing but my own thoughts to push me.

During hilly tempos or intervals on the track, it feels like I'm holding my hand over the flame—pushing my body to the limit while my mind screams *stop*. But I keep pushing, allowing myself to ride the pain. It never gets easier, but when race day comes, I know I have a mental edge that others on the start line don't.

— *Connor*

DATE	

Double Days

Double days are when you train twice in one day. Sometimes you need them for increasing training volume with a limited schedule. Sometimes you need them to get in two different types of runs in the same day. Sometimes you have a workout scheduled, and a friend asks you if you want to run . . . so you decide that running twice that day is worth it for the opportunity to catch up with a friend.

— *Adam*

DATE

DATE

DATE

DATE

DATE

Enemy Lines

Have you ever noticed that running changes how you conceptualize distance? When I was younger, even relatively short car trips felt like they took an eternity. For example, I grew up in a small town called Minooka, in the southwest suburbs of Chicago. Channahon was the town next to us and our sports rivals during grade and junior high school. Minooka and Channahon, though adjacent to one another, felt far apart. I wasn't a runner at that age, but the even the thought of running from my house to the town of Channahon would have been blasphemous.

Today while visiting my hometown, I ran from my parents' home to Channahon and back. The round trip took me less than an hour. I thought about my former self and telling him that I ran from home to Channahon. It put a smile on my face. If only that little boy could see me now!

— *Adam*

DATE

Walking Blues

I had the walking blues today—the walking-when-I-should-be-running blues. A couple of miles into a six-mile run, my back began to bother me. Soon every step sent a jolt of pain through my back. I have been there before; it happens when my hamstrings get tight, which happens when I don't stretch them. (Which is pretty much never.)

I tried stopping and stretching, but it wasn't enough. I had no choice but to walk home. Because I had not allocated enough time for the slower pace, I was forced to take a route along the shoulder of a busy road during rush hour traffic while it was snowing. I briefly felt sorry for myself, trudging along, keeping a wary eye out for the cars rushing by, and trying not to slip on the ice under the snow.

And then I got over it. I remembered I get to choose my response to things outside of my control. I decided to settle myself down and walk on.

Sometimes a run becomes a walk. When this happens, and if I can remind myself to feel grateful that I am getting to move, feeling the earth under me, I am able to walk past my blues. When I consider the people in the world who would give anything to walk even a few steps, I come back to where my feet are and am happy to walk on.

I'll see you further on up the road . . .

— *Jim*

Breathing Fire

Cool air fills my lungs
As it burns through my body
Fire breathes inside me

— *Adam*

All Winners

Running fast doesn't always feel fast. Sometimes running hard can make a workout feel longer, even though you're covering more ground. Challenging the body and mind isn't as easy as letting go and allowing your body to naturally dictate the effort required. In all cases, fast or slow, or somewhere in between, we're doing what we love. We're all winners!

— *Adam*

DATE

DATE

DATE

Hard, Simple Work

Before enlightenment, chop wood and carry water.
After enlightenment, chop wood and carry water.

—Zen proverb[6]

My motivation to run is driven by excitement for my next big race or the goal of chasing my next personal record (PR). But the daily life of a long-distance runner is about more than chasing shiny objects. It's about the process, the journey, and the trial of miles.

Our improvement comes not from one great workout or from one perfectly executed race but by doing the hard, simple work day in and day out.

Chop wood and carry water—the path to becoming our best selves is long and hard, but that's exactly why it's worth the grind.

— *Connor*

TIP

Motivation is essential to accomplishing huge goals. When you set out to achieve your running goals, identify your motivations ahead of time so that you have a strong foundation to rely on when things get tough.

Running Out of Daylight

There is a point sometime during September when my evening run becomes a race against twilight. I always lose. Within a two- or three-week period, I am starting my run at the same time, but it is already dusk. By November, all my weekday runs take place in the dark.

After taking a couple of years away from the corporate world, I am back at a desk and enjoying it. One of things I miss, however, is the freedom to run during daylight. During the past two years, a good part of my life seemed to revolve around deciding where Michelle and I would eat breakfast and at what time we would run. It was a pretty good life!

But today, Saturday, the weather was awful. The temperature was in the high 20s; there was a strong east wind, and last night's heavy rain was slowly turning into snow. I was still ecstatic at the chance to run during daylight, however. Michelle and I ran for an hour, and then after she returned home, I continued on for another hour through the deserted woods. I didn't care about my pace or being cold or if the snow would begin to accumulate. I just wanted to run and run and run under the gray sky.

I'll see you further on up the road . . .

— *Jim*

PART III
Flowy

Flowy

THIS IS IT! This is the feeling I often long for but rarely realize. It's that feeling when everything comes easily, it's all fluid, and you could quite literally run all day. Nothing feels forced and everything is in alignment. All is right in mind, body, and soul!

— Adam

| DATE |

DATE

DATE

DATE

DATE

As Good as It Gets

There is a perfect moment on a summer evening when the fireflies rise out of the grass, floating up into the air, their lights winking on in the deep dusk. There are maybe two minutes between deep dusk and full-on dark when the fireflies are rising. When I see them in that moment, forget about everything else, and stay present with the fading light and the glowing fireflies, that moment is about as good as it gets for me.

When I am running and I forget about my time, my creaky legs, and my form and just get to *flowy*, that's as good as a run gets.

I'll see you further on up the road . . .

— *Jim*

DATE

It's Jazz

The singer Van Morrison once said, "The theory is that you don't play a song the same way twice because it's jazz. That's where I'm coming from."[7] It feels to me the same thing is true for running.

At one level, all we do is throw on a pair of shoes and go out again and again. Yet every time it is different. There are good runs, bad runs, meh runs, and sometimes runs that combine all three.

Today I had just a glimpse of what Adam calls "flowy," where arms and legs feel like they're unspooling and suddenly floating without effort. But as the Zen saying goes, "When you think you have found it, you have lost it." As soon as I thought *flowy*, it was gone.

Every run is the same yet so different, and that is the joy and the challenge and what brings me back to the next run.

I'll see you further on up the road . . .

— *Jim*

TIP

Prioritize diversity in your running regimen. Incorporate easy runs, hill sessions, interval work, and speed work across a variety of training surfaces. It will make you a much more well-rounded runner!

Can't Wait

One of the joys of running is being able to explore new places. Today I'm on my honeymoon in South Carolina, and rather than running on the beach, I went inland and ran through the coastal forest. Coming from arid northern Arizona, I was excited to see the diversity of tree species and to look for mushrooms! It was one of those special runs where, despite the thick humid air and rivulets of sweat pouring down my body, I eagerly anticipated what lay ahead of me at each turn.

I already can't wait to see what tomorrow's run has in store.

— *Connor*

DATE

DATE

DATE

175

Churning

Legs tired, lungs burning
Soul full, heart yearning
Each adventure, always learning.

— *Adam*

_____

_____

_____

_____

_____

_____

_____

_____

_____

_____

_____

_____

Ever Improving

A number of factors have led to my love of trail running. One of the most basic is this: the trails ebb and flow in the same way that life ebbs and flows.

Ups and downs.

Highs and lows.

Successes and struggles.

Always learning, ever improving!

— *Adam*

Breathing, Running

For the last couple of years, I have been doing breathing exercises for five minutes a day. According to the app I use, I have practiced for 50 hours, including a stretch of 181 days in a row. I learned how hard it is to take one good breath and how hard it is to stay with the breath in the moment.

Running is like breathing. It seems so simple and can be done on autopilot. Yet the more I study running, the more I realize how much more I can learn and improve. Just like my breathing exercises, where I might struggle to get just one moment of *flowy* breathing, a run can be a journey full of unwelcome effort. My mind and body are two beings, disconnected and full of grumbles directed at the other being. And then without warning, the niggles and distractions drop away, and I am just running. That one moment is worth all the others; it can linger for hours afterward and propels me out the door tomorrow.

I'll see you further on up the road . . .

— *Jim*

Pure, Cold Bliss

There are few things I love more than a run on a cool, crisp morning. I feel an unexplained joy before my run begins as I shake my legs to stay warm, blow hot air into my hands, and sip a hot cup of coffee while watching my breath dissipate in front of me. Pure bliss!

— *Adam*

DATE

DATE

179

Friendly Gear

Having the right gear makes all the difference on a run.
I can run for hours when I have the right gear.

I get very attached to my gear. I bought two identical
winter running jackets, so I could wear the second one if the
first one was still wet from the previous day. Somehow I've
worn one more than the other and noticed it has developed
holes on the inside of both pockets. The pockets are now
nearly unusable, and I have been thinking about patching
them so I don't have to go through the stress of finding that
next perfect jacket. Plus, I like that the jacket has become
overused—it's like an old dependable friend and I'd miss it.

I'll see you further on up the road . . .

— *Jim*

DATE _____

_____

_____

_____

_____

_____

_____

_____

_____

_____

_____

_____

_____

DATE

DATE

The Sweet Escape

Running has always been an opportunity for me to "escape," but usually that means escaping from my daily worries, work, or simply being on my phone.

Lately, though, running to escape has taken on new meaning: I'm incredibly grateful for the chance to get outside each day and observe the world outside my home. To feel the warmth of the sun on my skin and smell the dry pine needles decaying on the forest floor has become its own journey.

— *Connor*

DATE

Velocitized

When I was traveling a lot for my job, I made up a word about how it made me feel: *Velocitized*. The word described how I was always in movement either getting ready to go somewhere, going somewhere, or getting ready to leave and go to the next place. This feeling continued until I was exhausted and only wanted to be at home. But once I was home, I'd become restless and want to be going somewhere again.

I sometimes feel the echoes of *velocitized* when I am running. When I haven't run for a bit, I keep thinking about the next run. When I am running, moving feels good, and sometimes I want to go on and on until my legs fail.

When I get back home, I am happy and peaceful until the restlessness slowly steals in, and I think about the next run.

The difference between running and traveling for work is that when I was traveling for work, I never arrived. I was always in the wrong place trying to get to somewhere else. With running, in those moments when my legs loosen and I get into *flowy*, then I am home, at peace, and happy.

I'll see you further on up the road . . .

— *Jim*

Happy Heart

Snow melts all around
Revealing the dirt below
My heart is happy

— *Adam*

Silver Linings

The mountains in winter present challenges for running. The typical trails I run on are covered in snow, and I'm relegated to running more frequently on bike paths and roads. Though I don't enjoy those as much, I realized today what a blessing they are. I'm fortunate that the weather conditions push me to run new routes and see places I wouldn't normally seek out. It's a gentle reminder that even when I think something is less than ideal, there's always a silver lining!

— *Adam*

DATE

Life

Things moving on by
Bikes, runners, birds in the sky
Life is all around

— *Adam*

Sunset

Sunset is a profoundly beautiful moment. The day is winding down; there's a feeling of calm in the air. And when you combine those with the feeling of running free, side by side with a beautiful alpine lake, the peripherals fall away and it's just you and the earth in front of you . . .

— *Adam*

DATE

Dog Days

What do dogs think about when they're running?

On some days, running is a time for me to think intensely and work out problems that have been nagging me in the back of my mind. Other days, running is the opposite: a delightful daydream on my feet in which active thinking is whittled down to concentrating on my next step, my next breath, or the next turn in the trail.

Regardless of my mindset, I rarely take the time to appreciate the act of running *while* I'm running. I'm either too caught up in my mind or not thinking consciously at all. And that's where I can learn from my dog, a fluffy white border collie mix. I'd like to think he appreciates every second on the trail or the road. Not worried about the work that needs to be done today or the race coming up next month—just boundless enthusiasm and gratitude to be running *right now.*

— *Connor*

TIP

A local running club is a great place to meet training partners and other people who share the same passions as you.

DATE

DATE

Found in Nature

Bounding down the trail
One foot after the other
Lost in my mind
Found in nature . . .

— *Adam*

DATE

DATE

Through Puppy Eyes

We'll be getting a new chocolate lab puppy in a few weeks, and I've been told to look forward to watching how a puppy learns about the world around her. Every new experience has its own wave of sights, sounds, and smells, and the puppy eagerly drinks it all in.

This has made me consider how I look at those same experiences. I come to them with preconceived notions, expectations, and distractions. *I've run this trail hundreds of times. I just need to get this workout over with. I have a lot of work that needs to be done when I get home.*

How different would those runs be if I experienced them through the eyes of a puppy?

— *Connor*

DATE

Joy in the Journey

I don't remember races as much as I remember training for them. For me, the joy is truly in the journey.

Last weekend Michelle and I ran with Connor on the morning of his wedding. On a beautiful fall morning, we ran on a favorite trail of ours, stopping to observe a red-tailed hawk perched over a creek bed, and then going on to our favorite breakfast spot. We will remember that run for a long time. I'll see you further on up the road . . .

— *Jim*

DATE

Freedom

Running is freedom. My soul running free, my heart running free, my legs running free. When the run begins, the world melts away . . .

— Adam

DATE

_____

_____

_____

_____

_____

_____

_____

_____

_____

_____

_____

TIP

Do you find yourself obsessed with the amount of mileage you are running? Consider training on a time-based schedule to alleviate those pressures and enhance the quality of your workouts!

DATE

DATE

The Running Dichotomy

I'm a social person, but I also truly value my alone time. Running is a dichotomy in that way: a fun and social experience, but also an incredibly therapeutic opportunity to work through your thoughts and feelings on your own.

So which is better? Each day is different, so I believe the answer is ever-changing.

Today I ran with a friend who was having a rough weekend. He was dealing with car problems, unexpected expenses, and getting called into work on a Saturday. But nothing seems to make our life challenges dissipate like sharing some miles and quality conversation out in this beautiful planet we call home.

— *Adam*

DATE _____

_____

_____

_____

_____

_____

_____

_____

_____

_____

_____

_____

_____

DATE

DATE

Choose Silence

We live in a hyperconnected world where, perhaps for the first time in human history, we have to actively choose silence. I was reminded of this last night while watching a documentary called *Honeyland* about a woman in north Macedonia who has almost nothing. No phone, no TV, no electricity. Throughout the film, she was shown sitting in utter silence in her small home with nothing but a flickering gas lamp and her cats for company. It made me wonder what am I missing by filling every available second with some form of mental stimulus?

Even when I'm physically alone, I have a constant unconscious urge to take advantage of the dead time by checking my phone or listening to a podcast.

The one time a day that this isn't true is during my run. I always leave my phone at home, allowing me to disconnect from everything other than the thoughts in my mind and the trail beneath my feet. Admittedly, this is a small step toward mental balance, but even a few miles of mind wandering leaves me feeling refreshed.

— *Connor*

Abundance

Single track dirt trails
Overflowing heart and soul
What else do I need?

— *Adam*

_____

_____

_____

_____

_____

_____

_____

_____

_____

_____

_____

_____

_____

_____

TIP

In order to become a mentally stronger runner, it's important not to shy away from tough conditions during training. You may not want to run on a cold, windy day, but you will be better for it!

Hope for Cranes

Standing outside my car, I thought I saw some sandhill cranes. It's hard to distinguish them from Canada geese, and the trick is to listen for their distinctive call. But I was by the local train station while a train was coming. By the time the train had passed, the birds were gone.

As I drove away, I saw big waves of the birds overhead. There is a week in March when the sandhill cranes reappear, moving north as the temperature warms. Seeing the cranes is special. It means that, while spring in the Midwest is still far off, I have come through the winter and there is hope—hope for spring, hope for summer, and hope for what lies ahead. I'll see you further on up the road . . .

— *Jim*

DATE

DATE

_____

DATE

_____

The Plovers and I

The plovers and I
scamper from the rising tide.
Our tracks disappear . . .

— *Connor*

| DATE |

A Midwest Spring

During my run yesterday, I heard sandhill cranes overhead. Their sound is like no other, and at first, they often sound like the distant honking of Canada geese. Unlike geese, however, the calls persist as they edge across the sky. It cheered me to hear them. It was a warm, windy spring day, and it felt as if the sandhill cranes were dragging spring behind them.

Chickadees chirped from the woods, making their spring calls. The first one made a high, sweet whistle and then another nearby answered—a call-and-response rhythm. It sounded like they were saying, "Where are you?" and then, "I am here." The back and forth was a lovely, simple sound.

Running and listening, especially to the birds, connects me to the world. The Midwest spring is a tug of war, summer and winter contesting the thawing earth. Gradually summer wins more and more of the contests but never as soon as I would like. Yesterday the birds told me that while summer lay some ways off to the west, it is coming, and that message kept me looking up and beaming at the bright blue sky.

I'll see you further on up the road . . .

— *Jim*

Thaw

February thaw
The gutters and I are flowing
In the afternoon sun

— *Jim*

For Love of Running

It's Valentine's Day . . . a day to celebrate love! I love
my family and friends, my dog, and everyone who has
supported me in my life.

But what do I love to *do*?

Cupid must have been wearing running shoes when
he struck me with his arrow.

— *Adam*

| DATE |

Shelter

There is a scene in the *Odyssey* where Odysseus is shipwrecked at night. Having barely survived, he finds himself on a beach, soaking wet and afraid of freezing to death. Despite the dangers lurking in the woods, Odysseus enters and finds two olive trees growing together. Under their dense shelter, he buries himself in a pile of leaves, "enough to cover two men over, even three, / in the wildest kind of winter known to man . . . / and Athena showered sleep / upon his eyes . . . sleep in a swift wave / delivering him from all his pains and labors . . ."[8]

For me, running, at times, is like Odysseus's bed of leaves under the sheltering olive trees. It restores me and is like a waking sleep—that place of deep comfort where even the wildest winter cannot pierce me.

I'll see you further on up the road . . .

— *Jim*

TIP

Run your easy runs easy, and your hard runs hard. Too many athletes fall into the trap of running at the same pace for most of their workouts.

Sanity

> Empty streets and trails ...
> my daily escape from quarantine
> keeps me sane.

— *Connor*

DATE

DATE

DATE

I Long

Although I long for
summer's warmth, I know I'll miss
the snow-covered Peaks.

— *Connor*

DATE _____

_____

_____

_____

_____

_____

_____

_____

_____

_____

_____

_____

_____

_____

_____

_____

_____

_____

The Gift of Songs

I heard robins during my run today. They have returned earlier than usual, and it was cheering to hear them. The sound was a happy little surprise and exactly one of the gifts running gives me. It was sleeting and raining, but the robins' song seemed to insulate me.

I struggled mightily on the run, however. I had dead legs and no energy. My mind was also weak, and I struggled to push myself. Difficult runs like this are also gifts because they show me where I am weak and instruct me on how to get better. I am grateful!

I'll see you further on up the road . . .

— *Jim*

DATE

DATE

DATE

217

DATE

DATE

Stripped Down

I was recently reflecting on the many ways that running has changed my life today, and I realized that if I had to condense it down to one thing, it's this: it has allowed me to discover who I really am.

Running long-distance races and expeditions inevitably forces me into situations where I am stripped down spiritually, mentally, physically, and emotionally. It's in those moments that I see how I am able to deal with the most adverse of circumstances. Without that experience, and the extreme highs and lows I've been through, I wonder—would I truly know who I am?

— *Adam*

DATE

Gifts of Running

When Michelle and I had a lake house set on a hill overlooking the water, I was fond of standing on our deck at night and listening to mysterious sounds in the woods and looking at the stars. Sometimes during the fall, I would hear geese on the wing in the dark. Moving from one spot to the next on the lake, their haunting calls emerged out of the blackness and washed up the hill. Their song made me restless, as I was standing on the deck, feeling the cold air hinting at a frost, and I wanted to be out there too, moving along in the night.

Last night while running in the dark, I first heard and then saw a few geese directly overhead, heading north, honking, and silhouetted by the hazy half-moon. *This is why I run,* I thought.

I never know what beautiful gift a run will give me. While my runs don't always bring a gift like the geese, it happens often enough that I begin every run feeling a bit like a kid at Christmas, excited to see what is under the "tree."

I'll see you further on up the road . . .

— *Jim*

Awaits Below

Upside down mountain . . .
I descend the canyon's rim.
What awaits below?

— *Connor*

Humbling

The wind is howling
But the mountains are calm
A dichotomy of nature
Surrounds me on all sides
Humbling me in its grandeur

— Adam

DATE _____

_____

_____

_____

_____

_____

_____

_____

_____

_____

_____

_____

Mountaintops

Today I summited Peavine Peak, the highest peak in Reno, Nevada. I've summited it many times before, but this was my first one of 2020. I did so with my coaching client Valerie. She had never summited before, so I was excited to share the moment with her.

There are few feelings as great as a mountaintop experience (literally, in this case), but I've found an equal joy in sharing it with someone else. The same is true of running. Is there any runner who you introduced to the sport? Maybe in some way you feel responsible for helping them cultivate a lifelong passion. It feels fulfilling to play even a small role in guiding someone to an activity that becomes a fruitful part of their life. Sharing a mountaintop together is much the same!

— *Adam*

DATE

Shortening the Miles

My wife Michelle is injured and unable to run. I miss our runs together. She is my wife, my life partner, and my running companion. Our runs have taken us up and down mountains in Death Valley, along the coastal headlands of Marin County, and across countless miles under the wide-open skies of the Midwest. We have talked for hours on these runs, arrived home, and then talked some more.

There is a Gaelic saying "Two shorten the road," and it's true for running. Sometimes a solo run can feel farther than a hundred-mile race, stretching out forever into the distance. When the anticipation of a solo run feels this way, I resist taking even one step out the door. I begin to long for some unexpected event that would allow me to sacrifice the run without actually admitting that I chose not to run because it was too tough to run alone.

In those moments, I wish for a *flowy* run that features not just a physical *flowy* feeling but the *flowy* of being connected with Michelle, talking, and hardly noticing the miles dropping away. Yes, there are times when it's nice to run alone, but running with Michelle is another reason why I run—to feel the *flowiness* that comes from being truly connected.

I'll see you further on up the road . . .

— *Jim*

Waiting

Clouds cling to the Peaks . . .
impatiently, I wait for
winter's snows to melt.

— *Connor*

Squall

Snow is abounding
Flakes landing on my face
Ice crunching below

— *Adam*

_____

_____

_____

_____

_____

_____

_____

I Shall Have Some Peace

One hazy summer, when I was a boy, my dad offered to take my siblings and me for ice cream cones if we could memorize poems of his choosing. Ice cream cones were a rare treat for us, and we were all in. The poems-for-ice-cream program went on all that summer.

One of the poems we memorized was "The Lake Isle of Innisfree" by William Butler Yeats. It's about a place of solace and restoration. It goes in part like this:

> Nine bean-rows will I have there, a hive for the honey-bee,
> And live alone in the bee-loud glade.[9]

Go back and reread those lines aloud. Don't they flow beautifully? That flow, where one word connects to the next and the next, is how a run can feel. Which leads me to another line from the poem: "And I shall have some peace there."[10] I'll see you further on up the road . . .

— *Jim*

DATE

DATE

What Trails?

Springtime in the mountains gives me a certain feeling. It's the joyous feeling of trails opening, flowers blooming, and endless sun spanning the sky. On spring days, I find such happiness by heading to familiar trails I haven't been able to run on all winter and seeing if the snow has cleared off.

Usually the first couple weeks of spring involve running on partially snow-covered trails, but then slowly it eventually all melts away. I call one of my favorite early-season running pastimes "What trails are open for business?"

— *Adam*

DATE

Best Run Ever

Runners treasure their PRs. These days I find myself thinking about another acronym: BRE. It stands for "best run ever." We would all define our BRE differently, but for me, it wouldn't be a race, even if I ran well. My BRE would be a long, gentle run with Michelle and full of scenic stops along the way to admire a hawk or the view.

I remember once stopping on a crisp fall morning, when the world was quiet and still, and hearing the sound of leaves falling after a hard frost. The leaves made a soft pitter-patter as they landed on the ground, sounding like a soft summer rainfall. We stood there in wonder, listening quietly, savoring a few beautiful moments.

If I had to pick just one BRE, it would be the Dipsea Trail run Michelle, Connor, and I did a couple of years ago. I had long dreamed of running it. We vacationed that year in Mill Valley California, choosing a hotel close to where the Dipsea begins. We ran from Mill Valley to Stinson Beach where we ate lunch. Our run was full of stops and beautiful sights and wonder and, as an old neighbor used to say, "Happy happy."

I'll see you further on up the road . . .

— *Jim*

Just Run!

While reading the final book in Frank Herbert's *Dune* series, I came across this quote: "Many things we do become difficult only when we try to make them intellectual subjects."[11]

As runners, we often spend mental energy fretting about things like having the right shoes, using a specific recovery modality, finding the perfect workout, or running at exactly the right pace. However, the beauty of running is in its simplicity. We become faster by getting out the door and putting in the miles day after day after day.

Days turn to weeks, weeks turn to months, months turn to years, and eventually we're better versions of ourselves.

No need to worry about today's pace, shoes, or heart rate . . . just go out and run.

— *Connor*

Choose Adventure

Oftentimes, while running on trails with a friend, we will arrive at a fork. One of us will ask, "Should we take the way we know or see where the new one leads?"

Familiarity versus adventure—which do you prefer?

Does it depend on the day, the moment, or perhaps who you're with?

— *Adam*

DATE

DATE

DATE

235

DATE

DATE

Thinking Thoughts

My mind always wanders on a run. It's my time to think through the many things happening in life. I can sort out my thoughts, work through struggles, and dream the biggest dreams. My motivation is never greater than when I am running.

As someone who rarely listens to music during a run, I find it interesting that on the random occasion that I do, these same thoughts happen. It's like the power of the run drowns out all the other (literal) noise.

— *Adam*

DATE

Here, There, Everywhere

I heard the February cardinals this week. Winter in the Midwest is quiet for birdsong, but sometime in early February, the cardinals will begin to sing shortly after sunrise. Although the cold air tells me we are still locked in winter, the cardinal sings a song of hope.

I was not quite done with my run one day, when I heard the cardinal, and it cheered me enormously. In its song I could hear every song sung between now and June, when both the summer and song of the swallows arrive.

The earth is turning, turning, turning in its forever rhythms, and I am here for just a short while. Running reunites me with these rhythms, and in that moment of hearing February cardinal song, I am there and I am also in June, and I am in every moment between now and then.

I'll see you further on up the road . . .

— *Jim*

Snow

The mountains are fluffy
With the glow of white snow
Soft pillows below

— *Adam*

Dry Dirt

Dry dirt. That was all it took to make my day.

Today I ran on the trails of Verdi, a town just across the Nevada border, close to Tahoe. Every time I get in a good trail run after having trained on pavement for a while, it feels like such a treat. Absence makes the heart grow fonder!

— *Adam*

DATE

Sun Dappled Leaves

Late September
Late afternoon run
Making sure
I remember the shadows
of sun dappled leaves
Wishing
this could go on forever . . .

— *Jim*

If the Shoe Fits

Runners obsess. We obsess about runs done, partially done, and not done. About upcoming races, about the last mile split, about the weather. But if you want to get a runner talking, just ask her about her shoes. There is nothing as personal as their shoes.

We live in a golden age of running shoes where every form of shoe is available. There are minimalist shoes that resemble sandals—in fact, some *are* sandals. Other shoes are enormous shoes that feel like you're running on pillows. My strong preference is for a brand of shoes that fall into the pillow category called Hoka. They work for me, and that is all I care about.

When I ran yesterday, it was cold and wet, and I ran in a pair of Brooks Ghosts that are waterproof and made with Gore-Tex. They work really well for running in cold, wet weather. But my feet, so accustomed to their Hoka pillows, were aching well before I finished the run.

I now find myself obsessing about whether I should buy a pair of waterproof Hokas. I probably will. After all, I am a runner.

I will see you further on up the road . . .

— *Jim*

Blue Skies, Smiling

There's a saying in Tahoe that goes, "West shore is the best shore." Living in Tahoe City, I'm on the western shore of the lake, so (unsurprisingly) I tend to agree with that statement.

Today I went for a run on the bike path that runs alongside Lake Tahoe. The sky was stunningly clear and completely blue, and I couldn't help but be filled with immense gratitude for seeing it. I always strive to feel grateful for every run because running is not only my greatest passion, but it's my life's calling. But every now and then, the beauty I see all around me on a run makes it impossible for that gratitude to remain dormant; I can't help but smile!

— *Adam*

DATE _____

_____

_____

_____

_____

_____

_____

_____

_____

_____

_____

_____

DATE

DATE

247

DATE

DATE

A Bit Better

Do you have a place where you put your keys when you get home? I do—but only kind of, sort of. I have three or four places I might put them. I then sometimes get frustrated searching for them when I haven't put them in any of the usual places. Those places are my reliable, safe, and comfortable spots.

Running is like that for me. It's where I go to do battle with my problems, doubts, and fears.

It's where I go to reconnect to the earth and its glorious rhythms.

It's where I go to find who I'm going to be.

It always leaves me feeling a bit better.

I'll see you further on up the road . . .

— *Jim*

DATE

Fire Road

For every run where I get lost, or things don't go as planned, there's a run where I flow perfectly, or an unexpected decision creates an even more gratifying conclusion! Today's run was the latter.

I went for a short run on some trails I had run on before. I frequent this particular trail a lot, but I almost always start in a different location. I began running on the classic Emigrant Trail in Truckee, California. At a certain point, I turned and went uphill onto an intersecting trail. That trail paralleled a fire road, and so I turned onto the fire road, going back in the direction from whence I came. The fire road undulated up and down through the woods and, ultimately, brought me almost exactly back to where I started. I hadn't planned a loop, but it just happened to fall into my lap. I've found that for everything the trail takes from me, it gives back tenfold.

— *Adam*

TIP

Cross-training is an important piece to the overall health of a runner. Consider incorporating into your training plan activities like cycling, strength work, or yoga.

Racking Up the Miles

If you travel much, you might have a preferred airline—one where you have lots of frequent flyer miles. I prefer American Airlines. I have flown 2,549,634 lifetime miles on American, but I am not proud of this figure. It tells me there were too many trips, too many times away, too many early mornings.

However, I have no idea about my lifetime running miles. Whatever the number is, it sits with me quite differently than my air miles. Early mornings, evenings, running for more than twenty-four hours in one go: how wonderful each run has been. Today's run is a new trip, a journey to somewhere I have never been, even if it's just my well-worn route into the next town and back.

I'll see you further on up the road . . .

— *Jim*

PART IV
Cooldown

Mix It Up

My choice of where to run is often dictated by what sounds more fun: running on a go-to trail, meeting a friend somewhere, or exploring a new place. Today was different.

Do you ever run in a different place simply because you want to wear some of your other shoes? I did that today. Lately, I've been exclusively running trails, but I have a newer pair of road shoes that don't have a lot of miles on them. So I decided to have some fun in the new shoes and mix it up with a run on the Tahoe Trailways Bike Path. I headed westbound and thoroughly enjoyed running several miles alongside the lake. Sometimes mixing it up means prioritizing shoes over location!

— *Adam*

DATE

DATE

DATE

255

DATE

DATE

Zero Day

There's something to be said for a day off. Although the grind of getting a little better, day after day, is my favorite aspect of running, having a lazy zero-day feels incredibly refreshing. It's easy to fall into the trap of feeling guilty for a day off, but what makes following "the Way" so enjoyable is making the choice to put in the work each day. So even though I didn't become any fitter today, I'm even more excited to get after it tomorrow.

— *Connor*

DATE

The Hungry Ghost

Perhaps it's because Michelle and I are dieting, but I have been thinking about the concept of a "hungry ghost." The hungry ghost exists in some Buddhist traditions. In one version, it is a ghost whose desires cannot be satisfied. Condemned to forever seek satisfaction of its desires, the ghost unhappily wanders through the world forever eating and forever hungry.

Driving to work today, I found myself becoming a hungry ghost of running. Michelle and I had gotten out into the cold, dark 5:30 a.m. world and run five miles, finishing up at our local Starbucks. We walked home, still in the dark, holding our warm coffee and talking about various things, comfortable and happy to have begun the day together. Yet on my way to work, when driving by a path meandering through some woods, I found myself wanting to explore it.

This was not the first time I have wanted more. More miles, more outside, more wide-open sky. More moving, moving, moving. I felt my hunger pains and reminded myself to be happy and content that I had run.

I will see you further on up the road . . .

— *Jim*

Sing a Song

I rarely listen to music when I run, especially in races. On the other hand, I'm often singing songs regardless of the fact that I'm not listening to them! Today I had an easy shakeout run, so I started singing one of my favorite songs by Florence and the Machine: "Shake it out, shake it out, shake it out, shake it out, ooh whoa!"[12]

— *Adam*

More Time to Run

I had a day off and slowly entered the world today, beginning with a leisurely breakfast with my wife Michelle. Later, I sat in my recliner and began reading a nine-hundred-page novel about the Japanese samurai Musashi.

The day fell away, and I could have stayed inside reading. But then I thought about the many days to come where I will be inside working and looking wistfully outside. The next thing I knew, I was running into a stiff southwest wind feeling cold, happy to be moving, and wishing I had more time to run farther.

I'll see you further down the road . . .

— *Jim*

DATE

Ancient Reunion

Driving west this morning, I looked in my rear-view mirror and saw the sun rising—a giant red ball just over the horizon. I had intentionally slept in, planning to run in the evening. But the sun surprised me; while bustling about and getting ready for work, I hadn't sensed the rhythm of night turning to day.

Running (or walking) is the thing that connects me to the rhythm of the world. With my feet literally on the ground, I sense the world's rhythms: dawn, dusk, dark, the first red-winged blackbirds giving me hope winter is winding down, and the eerie cry of the sandhill cranes far above in the late November sky, going south and taking fall with them.

When I run, I sometimes believe that I can feel the earth shifting just a little bit into the next season. Running is the thing that reunites me with something ancient: the need to be outside and moving and flowing in rhythm with the world.

I'll see you further on up the road . . .

— *Jim*

Home

Running along Lake Tahoe today, I reflected on the realization that I *am home*. This place is where I was always meant to be. The senses and emotions can't be dulled, even with time, because the beauty is overwhelming. I've only lived here for three and a half years, but my soul has lived here much longer. I just needed to walk (or, more accurately, run) the path that would bring me here. Home.

— *Adam*

_____

_____

_____

_____

_____

_____

_____

_____

_____

A Short Hundred Miles

Perspective is everything. Running one hundred miles is incredibly far, but it's really just a bunch of shorter races wrapped into one:

> Running from one aid station to the next.
> Running until you see your crew again.
> Running until you get some more fruit and Coke.
> Running with the thought of a loved one in your mind.
> Running through breathtaking trails in a foreign country.

Your mind might not like the idea of running a hundred miles, but running one more mile, or taking one more step, is certainly doable . . .

— *Adam*

DATE

DATE

_____

_____

_____

_____

_____

_____

_____

_____

_____

_____

_____

_____

Forest Bathing

The Japanese have a practice called *shinrin-yoku* or forest bathing. The idea is that by spending mindful time in a forest, you can cleanse your mind and spirit.

I find that the best trail runs are a form of forest bathing . . .

Soaking in the smell of decomposing leaves and the sound of live ones rustling in the wind . . .

Focusing on exactly where to place each step on the rock-strewn trail . . .

Moving without thinking; every once in a while, thinking without moving . . .

Taking in the call of an owl, the sight of a neat mushroom, or the view of the mountains between a break in the trees.

— *Connor*

A Goldilocks Runner

In the story "Goldilocks and the Three Bears," a little girl wanders into the house of some bears and tries their three beds and bowls of porridge. Each time it is the third try that was "just right." I was a Goldilocks runner, where hardly any day was "just right." It was too wet, cold, rainy, dark, too anything but perfect. I'd use these reasons to not run, telling myself I'd make up the miles by running longer later in the week and then regret that I hadn't run.

This changed when I began training for ultramarathons. One fall day, my training schedule called for a five-hour run. It was rainy with thunderstorms lurking; I was tempted to defer the run. But I knew how much *not* running would bother me. Instead, I ran loops on the rolling hills by our house, so I could bail in case of lightning. The lightning stayed away, I completed the run, and it felt like a callous formed inside of me.

Today was a fierce winter day full of howling winds and temperatures plummeting into the teens. Michelle and I ran anyway. After five miles, I dropped Michelle off and ran another six. At some point I forgot about the weather and became lost in thought until suddenly the run was over. And now, listening to the wind moan, everything is just right.

I'll see you further on up the road . . .

— *Jim*

Who Runs the Farthest

There is a song by Joe Pug called "Hymn #35." Part of it goes like this:

> I am the disappointed kiss
> I am the unexpected harvest
> I am the old Kentucky home
> I am the son who runs the farthest . . .[13]

I like the line "I am the son who runs the farthest." It feels right to me. I am indeed the son who runs the farthest. That may be good; it may be bad—I don't know. I just know it feels good to run and (sometimes) it feels good to run the farthest.

I'll see you further on up the road . . .

— *Jim*

DATE

DATE

Nothing Special ... Just Everything

After moving halfway across the country, from Missouri to Arizona, and then being isolated for much of the year due to a pandemic, I've developed a keen appreciation for having the opportunity to share a run with others. On a trip back to Missouri for my wedding, I was able to share a delightful morning run with my mom and Jim on one of my favorite trails.

We didn't talk about anything special—just politics, the pandemic, and people. And we didn't see anything particularly special—just a couple mushrooms, a red-tailed hawk, and a tree growing on a wooden bridge (okay, maybe this was unusual). But the shared experience of spending an hour together on foot was something I'll remember and appreciate for a very, very long time.

— Connor

DATE

Mittens and Rabid Squirrels

When I was a kid, my dad warned my siblings and me about squirrels, telling us they could carry rabies. He'd throw stones at squirrels when they entered our yard. That warning struck fear in me one eventful day.

I walked by myself to school when I was in kindergarten, impossible as that is to believe. We didn't own a car, and my mom had four (eventually six) other children all my junior. At that age, I was already showing a dreamy disregard for belongings and constantly lost things. As a result, Mom warned me, "Jimmy, do not lose your mittens." Despite her warnings, one day I did lose a mitten. Terrified, I didn't say a thing and found it a week later, near the road, in the mouth of a dead squirrel. *Will I get rabies from touching my mitten?* Caught between rabies and the wrath of Mom, I opted for rabies, retrieved my mitten, and walked home.

Today, after finishing my run, I couldn't find a mitten. I had put them in my pocket while running, and now it was gone. I remembered the dead squirrel and wondered if history would repeat itself. It didn't. I double-checked my pocket and found the mitten nestled deep. Standing there, I felt as if Mom was shaking her head at me. Fifty years later; nothing had changed.

I'll see you further on up the road . . .

— *Jim*

Last Summer's Self

Running up Schofield
Bending into the wind
The weak winter sun taunts me
While across the road
Last summer's self appears
Gliding down the hill
Tan and fit, he nods
"I'll see you further on up the road," I say
And bend back into the wind

— Jim

DATE _____

_____

_____

_____

_____

_____

_____

_____

_____

_____

_____

_____

DATE

DATE

Warm Beds

I could have run today, but I didn't, and I regret it. The bed was warm, the hour was early, and I told myself sweet lies like "You can run tonight." Now it is tonight, and the evening has too many moving pieces: phone calls, dinner, being with family—too many things that I will do half-assed if I run. Even if I did run, I wouldn't be where my feet are. Instead, I'd be in too many places mentally, feeling I was half-assing everything, and then the run would simply be exercise.

It's hard to miss a run. That's the conversation I should have had with myself this morning. As mentioned earlier, Townes Van Zandt's line "Don't turn none away" is this year's theme. There's a crazy storm predicted tomorrow with rain, freezing rain, and snow. I will run . . . if I can.

I'll see you further on up the road . . .

— *Jim*

DATE _____

_____

_____

_____

_____

_____

_____

_____

_____

_____

Body Talk

One important lesson I've learned since I became a professional ultrarunner is that sometimes you need to listen to your body. It sounds straightforward, but when I have a training plan I'm adhering to, a missed workout can feel like a loss in many ways. However, I've come to realize that rest is a tool you can employ much the same way you would any other tool you have in your training repertoire.

Today I was supposed to get out for a run, but my body said, "I think a day off will do us some good." I listened. It's hard to listen like that, because I think, "Am I just being lazy?"

After training rigorously for several years, I now know the difference between needing rest and slacking. I'll almost never take a day off that I didn't already have designated as a planned rest day. My mind tells me not to. But once you know your body intimately, and understand what it needs, an extra rest day can be as productive as a great workout!

— *Adam*

Coffee and Co.

Morning run complete . . .
we settle in for coffee
and good company.

— *Connor*

The Run Not Taken

The run not taken. Until I run, there is always the run to be done: the run not taken.

Last night Michelle and I talked about what time we might run today. We agreed to try in the evening. Michelle wasn't sure she would run then but maybe.

It snowed overnight, and shoveling the driveway and moving in the winter air felt pleasant this morning. While shoveling, I saw a runner, a blur of light blue and black against the white gray of winter crossing the street. As I lifted a heft of snow, I wished I was running right then too.

Later, Michelle and I did find the time to go for a run; I forgot my asthma inhaler, struggled to breathe, and had to walk for a bit. It was not the run I had imagined while shoveling, but I showed up and once again was reminded of how special it is to simply breathe.

I'll see you further on up the road . . .

— *Jim*

Snow Going

Snowshoe running is the epitome of a great cross-training exercise. Sure, you're technically running, but you're running in deep, sometimes soft, snow, and it oftentimes feels like you're running in slow motion. Without snowshoes, you would sink up to your knees. Weirdly enough, snowshoeing reminds me that sometimes I need to slow down. The snow and the snowshoes force me to go slower, and in the process, I become acutely aware of the fact I'm doing what I love.

Don't be afraid to slow down every now and then— soak in the life around you!

— Adam

DATE

Control Freak

With the emerging outbreak of COVID-19, my spring racing plans have been canceled. Although I'm bummed I won't have the chance to run my first ultramarathon and enjoy a long weekend dedicated to running, this has been a humbling lesson in Stoicism, an ancient school of philosophy that stresses the importance of embracing one's fate. I can only control what's in my control, and unfortunately, whether or not a race is held is well outside of my control. What's within my control, though, is my training. And as long as running is still allowed, you better believe I'll be lacing up every day.

See you out there.

— *Connor*

DATE

Make Mistakes

While reading a teaching textbook today, I came across a nugget of research indicating that people learn more from making and correcting mistakes than from being right in the first place. The neuroscientific mechanism behind this insight is that calcium is released when we correct a mistake, and calcium facilitates an increase in the brain's neuroplasticity. In other words, being wrong helps us learn better than being right.

This knowledge has profound implications for us in all walks of life, including in our running as we prepare for races, workouts, or training in general. We should be open to taking risks and learning from the bad bonk or extra painful last interval that we might experience as a result. Ultimately, by expanding our comfort zones, we can become even smarter, stronger runners.

— *Connor*

New Trails

One of my mantras for this year has been "Take the new trail." I've been making an effort to follow trails I've run past but never followed. In following these "new" trails, I've been able to link up new trails, create fun loops, and explore completely new areas that I missed but were right in front of me all along!

Today, after taking a left turn I had seen a few times before, the prize for my curiosity was the summit of nearby Scott Peak . . . and one of the best views of Lake Tahoe I've ever seen!

— *Adam*

Digging the Well

Today was "one of those days." My stomach was giving me all sorts of issues starting at about three miles into the run—probably one too many cups of coffee this morning! I felt terrible for the entire run, but I powered through. Partially because I wanted to get a mental victory, but mostly because my wife dropped me off several miles away from home—I had no choice!

Afterward, I spoke to my good friend and coaching client, Jim, and he reminded me of something I tell all my athletes on a regular basis: "Every time you get through something tough, you dig your well deeper." Now my figurative well is deeper and better equipped to handle whatever challenge or obstacle comes next.

— *Adam*

DATE

DATE

DATE

Running Together Apart

Today I participated in the iRunFar Operation Inspiration Virtual Race. While a virtual run wouldn't normally appeal to me, this one was quite special. Thousands of runners from all over the world ran together in spirit and raised funds for the World Health Organization's COVID-19 Solidarity Response Fund. While we're living in an eerie time of uncertainty, it's reassuring to see the world come together for the good of one another. The running community is always supportive and never disappoints.

— *Adam*

DATE _____

_____

_____

_____

_____

_____

_____

_____

_____

_____

_____

_____

There's Always Tomorrow

Despite our amazing ability to track and record our runs (we are living in the golden age of running), we can only do so much to preserve a run. Whether we have a good or bad run today, it's gone as soon as we stop running. Tomorrow we begin again, and who knows what tomorrow will bring? Tomorrow doesn't care about our desires or training or how early five a.m. comes. Yet tomorrow gives us the chance to renew our efforts and find our *flowy*.

I'll see you tomorrow further on up the road . . .

— *Jim*

DATE

The Way

One of my all-time favorite books is *Musashi* by Eiji
Yoshikawa,[14] an epic that tells the life story of Miyamoto
Musashi, a Japanese samurai who was born in the 1500s.
Musashi is arguably the greatest swordsman in Japanese
history but not because of any single skill or talent he had. He
famously said, "If you know the way broadly, you will see it
in all things."[15] Essentially, he was an incredible swordsman
because he followed "the Way," meaning that every
experience in life was an opportunity to learn and grow.

In the novel, Musashi remarks upon the beauty and
precision with which another samurai cut a flower. This
attention to detail and desire to always improve is what
made Musashi a master.

What experience will you have today that can teach
you how to be a better runner?

— *Connor*

Toward March

> The fox tracks
> Disappearing in the melting snow
> Weakening but not yet
> Conceding
> Winter and I
> Push on
> Toward March

— *Jim*

Feeling Small

Today I came back from my run with a full heart. For the second time this year, I summited Peavine Peak, the highest point in the city of Reno at over eight thousand feet. When I got home, I said to my wife Karen, "There's something so fulfilling about standing on top of *any* summit."

For me, summiting has nothing to do with feeling a sense of accomplishment. In fact, the fulfilling part is really all about the acknowledgment of being such a small part of such a big, beautiful world. When I stand on that mountaintop, my perspective shows me how small I really am!

— *Adam*

DATE

A Slushy Regret

Do you ever think to yourself, "I should have run at a different time today?" Sometimes it's the temperature, precipitation, daylight, or any number of other reasons that unintentionally made your workout a bit harder. Well, my snowshoe run today had me asking myself, "Why did I run in the middle of the day?!"

The weather was impeccable and warmer than expected, which meant the snow was nice and slushy. Had I gone out early in the morning or later that night, it would have been frozen, making things a lot easier. Instead, my feet were frozen and my legs sopping wet from all of the slushy snow. But hey, sometimes an unexpected challenge out on a run is good.

While challenges seem tougher in the moment, facing them make us better humans when we're finished!

— *Adam*

DATE _____

_____

_____

_____

_____

_____

_____

_____

_____

_____

_____

Blizzard Pi

Pi Day in a blizzard! Are either of those food? Nope!

It was Pi Day (March 14, a day named after the mathematical constant pi or 3.14), and there was a snowstorm blasting snow all around me. But did I wish it were food? I mean, a piece of apple pie and a Dairy Queen Blizzard after the run does sound nice!

Running is such a mental sport. It takes a long period of time and experiences to cultivate the mental strength we need to succeed. As such, I like to mix in activities outside of running to help me to develop a stronger mental game.

Living in Tahoe City, California, I have immediate access to water. Lake Tahoe, the Truckee River, and a number of other dams and reservoirs are very close to where I live. These water sources are cold, even in the summer when the temperatures are really nice. So what happens when I finish up a run along the Truckee River? I wade waist deep into the river for postrun recovery! The cold water bites my skin at first, but after a few minutes, the pain subsides, and I am rewarded with healing and rejuvenation. The cold therapy is good for my body, but even better for my mind! So bring on the Pi Day blizzard; the cold never bothered me anyway (sorry, Elsa).

— *Adam*

Personal Worsts

I have reached a point in my running career where new PRs are unlikely and most likely PWs (personal worsts) lie ahead. I am okay with that. In some ways, it takes the pressure off, because I no longer have to beat myself up for not crushing a run. Now the goal is more about getting out and moving.

Today's run was one that, in the past, I would have beaten myself up about. It was cold and windy and dark, and I felt as if I were wearing concrete shoes. With only a mile left, I had to badly go to the bathroom, forcing me to walk the last quarter mile home.

No matter. I still got up at 4:45 a.m., got outside, and got moving; now I feel better for having done it. That is good enough. I'll see you further on up the road . . .

— *Jim*

DATE	

DATE

DATE

Deep Thoughts

Have you ever thought about the names of some of the trails you run on? Today I ran on a trail called "Drunken Deer," a popular trail in Truckee. Occasionally, I will spend the majority of a run delving into some random thought, and the origin of the trail name captured my imagination today.

That sometimes happens to me with common sayings. I ask things like "How did this saying come about? Who named this trail? Is there a great story behind it?"

That's why when people ask me, "What do you think about when you run?" the answer isn't always straightforward.

— *Adam*

DATE

Summer Morsels

When I was a boy, growing up in a house overrun with nine people and no air conditioning, the thermometer dictated the meals Mom made for dinner. On steaming hot days she would make BLTs (bacon, lettuce, and tomato sandwiches) for dinner, so she didn't have to turn on the oven. My six siblings and I would eat our BLTs outside off of paper plates loaded with Jays potato chips and watermelon wedges, the seeds of which we spat out, and they occasionally took root where they landed.

Hot summer days in the Midwest are tough, but like BLTs, they are to be savored. Today my wife Michelle and I ran in the hot summer afternoon. It was the first time this summer where my shorts became soaked with sweat, something that, though it feels absolutely wrong—my pants are wet!—signals a tough effort. And just like I reach back into my bottled memories of those hot summer childhood days, I wish I could bottle all this high-hot heat for a later gray November day when it's thirty-nine degrees and raining. In the meantime, I will enjoy every morsel of this summer.

I'll see you further on up the road . . .

— *Jim*

Embrace the Rain

Running in the rain is a funny thing. If you asked me,
"Do you enjoy running in the rain?" I would probably say
that I prefer running in cool temperatures with sunshine.
And though we get a lot of snow in the mountains, rain is
a relatively rare thing in Lake Tahoe.

Of course, it started raining on my run today. At first
the rain was light, and then it gradually got harder. As I
started getting wet, I initially hoped it would stop. But then,
at a certain point, I just embraced it. Every run on the
trails is symbolic of my joining of forces with nature, and
this just added to this symbiosis. I may have finished the
run cold and wet, but my heart was warm and happy!

— *Adam*

DATE

DATE

DATE

Running in Circles

Sometimes life circumstances can make running less than ideal. Weather, circumstances, time of day—all of these can impact how motivated we feel or how challenging a run will be.

The snow in Tahoe was covering most of the bike paths today, so I was relegated to running on some neighborhood roads, including a loop around a transit center. It made me think about my ultrarunning friend Stephanie, who works at the United Nations (UN) in Afghanistan. She regularly runs laps around the top of the UN building, because it's too dangerous to run elsewhere. As I ran around the transit center, I couldn't help but be grateful that I was able to run in such a beautiful place, regardless of how repetitive it was. Sometimes the most challenging runs are the ones that teach us the most!

— *Adam*

Heartbreak Hill

Mondays are usually a rest day for me. On this particular
Monday, however, I couldn't resist taking part in the
Heartbreak Hill Virtual Challenge, a run in honor of the
day the Boston Marathon was supposed to be run but was
canceled due to the pandemic. The challenge was organized
by my running sponsor, rabbit, and the goal was for everyone
participating to run at least 2.62 miles (an ode to the
marathon distance) and cover at least 91 feet of vertical gain,
the approximate climb of the infamous "Heartbreak Hill" of
the marathon. It's been a joy to see so many people in the
running community get creative with goals and challenges.
So even though it was my day off, I couldn't resist joining
the family in the challenge. I love that even when times are
tough, we can always find ways to stay connected!

— *Adam*

Date Night?

Today, my wife and I had a summit date night. As she described it, it was some "Type 2 fun!"—insufferable while doing it but, in hindsight, something you can't stop talking about afterward. We both surged up a two-mile climb with over twelve hundred feet of vertical gain. After cresting the summit, we spent a minute catching our breath while soaking in some amazing, panoramic views of Lake Tahoe, before cruising back down the mountain and to our car.

I sure am grateful to have a wife who considers that a "date!"

— *Adam*

Fly Like Superman

While running on an unfamiliar single-track trail the other day, I tripped, launching into the air, a vertical being now horizontal. Then WHAM! I crashed hard into the dirt, cursing. If I could curse, I was probably okay, I figured. And I was. But the fall knocked me off-center, and I was cautious for the next half-hour, hesitating and picking my way through the roots and rocks on the trail.

Later, I thought about what I learned from the run: when running a single-track, bring some band aids in case of a fall, practice a routine to recenter myself after falling, and, as always, be where my feet are.

In the meantime, I can't wait to get back out on that trail and learn how to run it well.

I'll see you further on up the road . . .

— *Jim*

DATE

DATE

Never Rest

Today my training plan calls for a rest day. Man, do I hate rest days. I become restless and adrift, desiring a feeling of moving forward—of being in motion. Michelle has wisely pointed out that this is why I need a training plan, because otherwise I don't take days off, and I slowly descend into poorer performance and increase the risk of injury.

There is a man in our town who is reputed to run a marathon distance each day. Occasionally I see him out on the road. He is often walking, head down, shuffling along. There, but for Michelle and Coach Adam, go I—such strong legs, yet such a weak a mind. That is the glory of my running journey: a battle with myself to get stronger physically and mentally (especially mentally). There is no ultrarun as hard as the one I run every day in my head.

I'll see you further on up the road . . .

— *Jim*

DATE

Home Course Advantage

One of the wonderful things about running is how our legs create our home course, that route you know deeply and intimately. The other day I ran on what I think of as my home course in Lake Geneva, Wisconsin: the path that runs twenty-two miles around the lake. It's a technical run full of roots and rocks and with abrupt transitions to smooth asphalt or someone's lawn. I have learned this path so well that I can safely run on it even in the deepening dusk on a fall evening as the path recedes into shadows and is full of leaf-covered obstacles.

It was a joy to run there again and find the path rising up to meet me, with all the familiar bits still there: the lurking pipe sticking up out of the ground within the first hundred yards, the loose flagstone by the old estate, and the spot where Michelle and I saw five scarlet tanagers on a cool May afternoon.

On and on we go, continually carving out our home course and our best place through streets and paths and trails, carrying bits of the past into the future.

I'll see you further on up the road . . .

— *Jim*

DATE

DATE

Unnecessary Obstacles

There is a line in Bernard Suits's book *The Grasshopper* about challenges: "Playing a game is a voluntary attempt to overcome unnecessary obstacles."[16] I have been thinking about this line and how it applies to running. Certainly running a race, be it a 5K or 50-miler, is an attempt to overcome unnecessary obstacles.

I was thinking about accepting unnecessary obstacles when I ran yesterday. I felt old and creaky, and I couldn't get warmed up. My workout called for two miles at a 5K race pace, and as much as I pushed, it felt as if I were running in mud. There was a part of me that wanted to quit and walk home, but there was another part of me that relished the challenge of navigating the conflict between my body and my mind.

I was able to see so much in my run yesterday. There will be the inevitable time when my body ultimately fails me, the future runs and races where I will struggle and still find wild beauty in the struggle, the understanding of how much running means to me so that even a "bad run" is painfully glorious. I will continue to pursue the challenge to be where my feet are and accept whatever there is in the moment. Running is the great crucible, continually refining me and helping me navigate myself. On I run, under a big blue sky filled with birds on the wing, until the run is over; then I begin again tomorrow, newly formed and ready for the next leg of the journey.

I'll see you further on up the road . . .

— *Jim*

Smelling the Barn (a.k.a. Conclusion)

Despite feeling as if they have nothing left in the tank, some runners nearing the final miles of a race find new energy and surge to the finish. Runners call this final push "smelling the barn" because horses often know when they are close to home and hurry to get there. While you are now at the end of this journal, we hope you have just begun to smell the barn and are surging toward a lifelong journey of running and writing.

If you are like us, there have been good days and bad days and perhaps days you took off and regretted it. The great thing about running and writing, though, is there is always tomorrow. Another day begins and so does your run and your time to reflect and write.

We encourage you to keep going, doing whatever works best for you, and continuing to grow as a runner, as a writer, and as a human being. For more encouragement, you can reach us at chasingtwilightjournal.com.

If you are in Lake Tahoe, Flagstaff, or the Chicago area, drop us a line and we would enjoy meeting you for a run.

If you are looking for a virtual running coach, Adam offers virtual coaching for runners at all levels, and you can reach him at adamkimble.com.

If you are looking for leadership coaching, Jim offers virtual leadership coaching, and you can reach him at jim@chasingtwilightjournal.com. You can also buy Jim's book on leadership, *Now You Will Excuse Me*, online at amazon.com, barnesandnoble.com, and other retailers.

ADAM

CONNOR

JIM

Adam Kimble is a professional ultrarunner, motivational speaker, running coach, race director, and amateur survivalist. Adam played Division I baseball at Bradley University prior to developing his passion for ultrarunning. After graduation, he ran his first ever 5K race near his hometown of Minooka, Illinois, in 2009, completed his first half-marathon in 2011, and completed his first ultramarathon (50K) in 2014. He has gone on to run the fastest known time (FKT) on the 171-mile Tahoe Rim Trail (37 hours, 12 minutes, and 15 seconds), completed a 60-day transcontinental crossing of the USA (2,500 miles), spent 60 days alone in the wilderness to become the winner of Discovery Channel's *The Wheel*, and completed a 31-day self-supported FKT across Great Britain.

He lives in Tahoe City, California, with his wife Karen and his dogter (dog-daughter) Sofi.

Connor Crouch is a forest scientist who is currently pursuing his PhD at Northern Arizona University in Flagstaff. Connor obtained an undergraduate degree in journalism, but not before realizing his passion for forestry rivaled his joy for writing. He researches how forest management can help restore forest ecosystems and enable them to adapt to a changing climate. When not looking for insects and mushrooms or camping for field work, Connor enjoys running the trails of Flagstaff, reading science fiction and fantasy, and spending time with his nonrunner wife Lyndsey and soon-to-be-runner dog Willow.

Jim O'Brien has worked in senior roles for a variety of asset management organizations, including London-based Henderson Global Investors, where he was a member of the executive committee and oversaw its US business for nine years.

Jim served as a trustee of the Henderson Global Funds board and as president of Henderson Global Funds, and he was a board member of THRE, a $20 billion joint venture between TIAA-CREF and Henderson. Jim also served as a board member of the Olson Company, a California-based homebuilder, and is currently the president of Aaron Equipment Company.

Jim enjoys reading, gardening, and ultramarathons as well as spending time with his wife Michelle and their children.

Acknowledgments

Adam Kimble | To my family, who is always so supportive of all of my endeavors, no matter how foreign they seem to them. Mom and Dad, saying "Thank you" will never be enough. Andy, you've been a better big brother than you could ever imagine. And Sofi, from the moment you entered our family as a puppy, you've taught me more about love than I could possibly imagine. I love you all so much.

To my incredible friends Josh and Kara, who would drop everything at a moment's notice to come and crew me at one of my races. Your selflessness inspires me every day, and I'm eternally grateful to have you both in my life. When Josh asked me to run my first 50K in 2014, he unknowingly set off a chain of events that would forever change my life. Love you both.

To my friend and coach, Peter Fain. I've learned so much from you both as an ultrarunner and as a coach, and I'm a more successful person today because of that. I strongly believe that everything happens for a reason, and when I saw your long hair and short shorts for the first time after moving to Tahoe, I knew I was destined to become your protégé. Thanks for everything, brother.

To our editor, James. Without your guidance and expertise through the writing process, this journal would not be the success that it is. Thank you so much for turning our work into something greater, my friend.

To Jim and Connor, I couldn't have enjoyed this journey with you two anymore than I did. Your writing inspired me to make mine better, and it was truly a joy to collaborate with you. Whenever you need a pacer or crew in the future, you know where to find me! *AK*

Connor Crouch | To Adam and Jim for being the greatest long-distance running and writing partners I could wish for. To write is to observe, and in my entries, I hoped to emulate your ability to always see the way, Jim. Writing is also never a solitary act, and I envy your boundless enthusiasm for sharing the sport of running with others, Adam.

To James, our industrious editor, for the countless hours you spent helping us become better writers. I'm sorry that after twenty-plus years of being in school and spending months with you editing, I never learned Chicago Style.

To my mom, Michelle, for showing me at a young age that early morning long runs in Chicago winters are possible. I may never have gotten into running if it weren't for you, and that deserves all the thanks in the world.

To Dad, Coleman, Maggie, and Lyndsey, for always cheering me on in running and in life.

To Hot Pie and Willow, for helping me slow down and appreciate the simple joys of our world.

Jim O'Brien | To Adam and Connor for graciously agreeing to come along with this passion project; it is immeasurably better for your work and your words.

To Karen Kimble and Lyndsey Crouch for giving up your time with Adam and Connor when they spent multiple weekends crewing at my ultras. And to Lyndsey, for contributing her artwork—thank you!

To our editor James, for making it seem effortless to work with three different and independent authors. I am grateful for your exact right words and the commitment you brought to making each entry the best it could be.

To Maggie, Colleen, Joe, and Claire for giving so generously of your time during my ultras. To Chrissie and Jimmy and Coleman: I'll see you at the next one!

To Sara Bordens, who ran with Michelle and me through the season of COVID and who helped create the WS 100 and the route known as JJ.

To my brother Peter and my sister Kathy for inspiring me as they run the races laid out for them.

To my former boss, Kelley Bergstrom, whose JMB-PMC three-mile race got me started running in 1983. Long may you run, Kelley.

Endnotes

1 Clare Gallagher, "Runner's High Haikus," *Trail Runner Magazine*, October 2017, 16.
2 Townes Van Zandt, "To Live is to Fly," recorded 1971–1972, track 8 on *Sunshine Boy: The Unheard Studio Sessions & Demos 1971–1972*, CD 1, Omnivore, 2013, compact disc.
3 Van Zandt, "To Live is to Fly."
4 See "The Diamond Sutra," *Journeys on the Silk Road*, 2019, http://journeysonthesilkroad.com/content/sutra.html; Barbara O'Brien, "A Famous Verse from the Diamond Sutra: A Bubble in a Stream," Learn Religions, last updated February 21, 2019, https://www.learnreligions.com/a-bubble-in-a-stream-450098; *The Sutra Book of the Greater Boston Zen Center*, edited and adapted by Josh Bartok (2019), 78, https://bostonzen.org/download/gbzc-liturgy-book/.
5 Ernest Hemingway, *A Farewell to Arms* (Scribner: New York, 1995), 107.
6 Ron Roth and Roger Montgomery, *The Sacred Light of Healing: Teachings and Meditations on Divine Oneness* (Lincoln, NE: iUniverse, 2007), 141.
7 For future reference, this came from an interview with Ritchie Yorke and the original quote was from this page (since moved): http://ritchieyorke.com/2015/04/21/an-interview-van-morrison/.
8 Homer, *The Odyssey*, translation by Robert Fagles (New York: Penguin, 1996), 5.36–37, 44–46.
9 W. B. Yeats, "The Lake Isle of Innisfree," *The Collected Poems of W. B. Yeats* (Hertfordshire, UK: Wordsworth Poetry Library, 2000), lines 3–4.
10 Yeats, "The Lake Isle of Innisfree," line 5.
11 Frank Herbert, *Chapterhouse: Dune* (New York: Penguin, 2019), 142.
12 Florence and the Machine, "Shake it Out," track 2 on *Ceremonials*, Island Records, 2011, compact disc.
13 Joe Pug, "Hymn #35," track 4 on *Nation of Heat*, Joe Pug, 2008, compact disc.
14 Eiji Yoshikawa, *Musashi* (New York: Kodansha, 2012).
15 Miyamoto Musashi, *The Book of Five Rings* (USA: Bottom of the Hill Publishing, 2010), 15.
16 Bernard Suits, *The Grasshopper: Games, Life and Utopia* (Peterborough, Ontario: Broadview, 2005), 55. First published 1978.

Made in the USA
Middletown, DE
26 November 2023